Love, Luxury and Beauty
in Classical Antiquity

Masterpieces from
The Museo Archeologico Nazionale
di Napoli

盛世爱情
意大利庞贝精品文物大展

盛世爱情

意大利庞贝
精品文物大展

LOVE,
LUXURY AND BEAUTY
IN CLASSICAL ANTIQUITY

Masterpieces
from
The Museo
Archeologico
Nazionale di Napoli

深圳市南山博物馆
　　　　　　　　编
意大利那不勒斯国家考古博物馆

文物出版社

图书在版编目（ＣＩＰ）数据

盛世爱情：意大利庞贝精品文物大展 ：中英对照 /

深圳市南山博物馆，意大利那不勒斯国家考古博物馆编

. -- 北京 ：文物出版社，2023.9

ISBN 978-7-5010-8123-3

Ⅰ . ①盛… Ⅱ . ①深… ②意… Ⅲ . ①博物馆－历史

文物－那不勒斯－图集 Ⅳ . ① K885.46

中国国家版本馆 CIP 数据核字（2023）第 120347 号

盛世爱情
意大利庞贝精品文物大展

LOVE, LUXURY AND BEAUTY IN CLASSICAL ANTIQUITY
Masterpieces from The Museo Archeologico Nazionale di Napoli

编　　　者：深圳市南山博物馆、意大利那不勒斯国家考古博物馆

责任编辑：智　朴

责任印制：王　芳

出版发行：文物出版社

社　　　址：北京市东城区东直门内北小街 2 号楼

邮　　　编：100007

网　　　址：http://www.wenwu.com

经　　　销：新华书店

装帧设计：雅昌（深圳）设计中心　冼玉梅

印　　　制：雅昌文化（集团）有限公司

开　　　本：889mm×1194mm　1/16

印　　　张：13.75

版　　　次：2023 年 9 月第 1 版

印　　　次：2023 年 9 月第 1 次印刷

书　　　号：ISBN 978-7-5010-8123-3

定　　　价：308.00 元

图录编辑   CATALOGUE EDITING

主　　编：戚鑫   *Chief Editor:* Qi Xin

副 主 编：刘昉   *Associate Editor:* Liu Fang

编　　委：黄海滨　郭岱伦   *Editorial Board:* Huang Haibin, Guo Dailun

内容整理：郭岱伦   *Content Editor:* Guo Dailun

英文校对：张熠   *English Proofreading:* Zhang Yi

展览组织与实施

意大利那不勒斯国家考古博物馆

总 策 划：保罗·朱列里尼

展览策划：玛丽娅露西亚·贾科

展览统筹：帕特丽夏·奇莱恩蒂

展览执行：斯蒂法尼娅·萨维亚诺

展 览 部：劳拉·福尔特　玛丽娅露西亚·贾科

展品保护：劳拉·福尔特　玛丽娅露西亚·贾科　弗洛丽安娜·米埃莱
艾玛努埃拉·桑塔尼埃罗乔瓦尼·瓦斯塔诺

展品修复：玛丽亚特蕾莎·欧培莱托

通讯联络：安东内拉·卡尔洛

宣传推广及社会教育：乔瓦尼·瓦斯塔诺

摄影档案：劳拉·福尔特

展览摄影：路易吉·斯宾纳

深圳市南山博物馆

总 策 划：戚鑫

展览统筹：刘昉

展览策划：黄海滨

展览执行：郭岱伦

展陈设计：冯时　方丹霞

视觉设计：陈思敏　林洁纯

宣传推广：张亚东　余秀清　陈婕　陈沫霖　刘晏鑫

社会教育：刘佳妮　郑曼　白之仑　邱烨　陈梓仪

展品管理：郭岱伦　郑宇　付梦钰

展览协助：王钒

中国文物交流中心

总 策 划：谭平

展览统筹：孙小兵

展览策划：冯雪　任正培

展览执行：孙天琪

CHINAMUSEUM INTERNATIONAL CO., LTD

总 策 划：钱茜

展览协调：埃莉奥诺拉·法莱赛迪、莎拉·巴勒莫

艺术总监：盖特·迪杰苏

展览设计团队

Eawe Project Co., Ltd：比安卡·戈梅里尼

渲　　染：埃马努埃拉·马加罗

平面设计：瓦莱里奥·斯皮内利

多 媒 体：贝尔纳尔多·伊拉奇、The Fake Factory、Hiflyfilm

翻　　译：李赛林　吴淑华　埃莉奥诺拉·法莱赛迪

媒体支持：意大利广播电视公司档案部

EXHIBITION ORGANIZATION AND IMPLEMENTATION

MUSEO ARCHEOLOGICO NAZIONALE DI NAPOLI

General Planning: Paolo Giulierini

Exhibition Curation: Marialucia Giacco

Secretariat: Patrizia Cilenti

Administration: Stefania Saviano

Exhibitions Office: Laura Forte, Marialucia Giacco

Conservation: Laura Forte, Marialucia Giacco, Floriana Miele
Emanuela Santaniello, Giovanni Vastano

Restoration: Mariateresa Operetto

Communication: Antonella Carlo

Exhibition Publicity & Public Education: Giovanni Vastano

Photographic Archive: Laura Forte

Photography: Luigi Spina

NANSHAN MUSEUM

General Planning: Qi Xin

General Coordination: Liu Fang

Exhibition Curation: Huang Haibin

Exhibition Production: Guo Dailun

Exhibition Space Design: Feng Shi, Fang Danxia

Exhibition Visual Design: Chen Simin, Lin Jiechun

Exhibition Promotion: Zhang Yadong, Yu Xiuqing
Chen Jie, Chen Molin, Liu Yanxin

Education & Public Programs: Liu Jiani, Zhengman
Bai Zhilun, Qiu Ye, Chen Ziyi

Objects Conservation: Guo Dailun, Zheng Yu, Fu Mengyu

Exhibition Assistance: Wang Fan

ART EXHIBITIONS CHINA

General Planning: Tan Ping

General Coordination: Sun Xiaobing

Exhibition Curation: Feng Xue, Ren Zhengpei

Exhibition Production: Sun Tianqi

CHINAMUSEUM INTERNATIONAL CO., LTD

General Planning: Qian Qian

Exhibition Coordination: Eleonora Falesiedi, Sarah Palermo

Artistic Director: Arch. Gaetano di Gesu

Exhibition Design Team

Eawe Project Co., Ltd: Arch. Bianca Gommellini

Rendering: Arch. Emanuela Magarò

Graphic Design: Valerio Spinelli

Multimedia: Bernardo Iraci, The Fake Factory, Hiflyfilm

Translations: Li Sailin, Wu Shuhua, Eleonora Falesiedi

Media Support: Rai Teche

序言一

当两种文化邂逅相逢，勇于相互了解，彼此欣赏时，它们就会迈出真正的一步，而这一步即是文化的进步。

如今，这项崇高的任务落在了中国和意大利的肩头。"盛世爱情——意大利庞贝精品文物大展"将于中国深圳市南山博物馆展出古希腊与古罗马时期的世界级艺术杰作。

那不勒斯国家考古博物馆非常荣幸，能以顶级水准参与到"一带一路"计划中，重循古丝绸之路，加强两国之间的交流。中国与意大利曾占据着古代世界最伟大帝国的中心位置，而当下又同为拥有最多联合国教科文组织世界遗产的国家。

在此，衷心感谢南山博物馆及 ChinaMuseum International 为本展览所作的精心策划与有力推动。我们希望，"盛世爱情——意大利庞贝精品文物大展"能够得到众多中国朋友的欣赏，增强我们两国之间的纽带关系。

心中有爱，目中有美，此美好愿景定将成真。

意大利那不勒斯国家考古博物馆馆长

保罗·朱列里尼

Preface I

When two worlds meet and have the courage to get to know and appreciate each other, they take that true step called cultural progress.

It is up to China and Italy to perform this noble task, through this exhibition, in the grandiose city of Shenzhen, of masterpieces that refer back to the world of classical Greece and Rome.

The MANN of Naples is profoundly honoured to trace, with a very high-profile operation, the new Silk Road, which retraces the ancient one, reviving exchanges between two countries that were the centre of the greatest empires of the ancient world and which today, together, have the largest number of UNESCO sites.

Thank you, therefore, to Nanshan Museum and ChinaMuseum International for the commitment and dedication provided for this exhibition, which we hope will attract large audiences and help strengthen relations between our counties.

It could not be otherwise if Love and Beauty reign.

Director of Museo Archeologico Nazionale di Napoli

序言二

众所周知，意大利是拥有最多世界文化遗产的国家，有着历史悠久、类型丰富的文化遗存。本次由南山博物馆携手意大利那不勒斯国家考古博物馆共同举办的"盛世爱情——意大利庞贝精品文物大展"，是我馆第三次举办体现意大利文化的展览，也是我馆贯彻"展现世界优秀文化"这一办展方向的又一个重要展览。

庞贝位于意大利的中西部，深受古希腊和古罗马文化的影响。由于1900多年前的维苏威火山喷发，将这座古城的历史定格在公元79年，也使得大量丰富多彩的文物得以原样保存。本次展览的展品均来自意大利那不勒斯国家考古博物馆，我们力图通过这些精美绝伦的雕塑、陶器、壁画和建筑物构件等不同类型的文物，重现出彼时庞贝城的盛世景象，让观众能够充分了解意大利的文化魅力。

近年来，南山博物馆持续举办了多个反映"一带一路"沿线国家人文历史的优质展览，得到了广大观众的认可。今后，我们将继续加强人类文明的交流互鉴，持续为粤港澳大湾区观众带来丰富多彩的文化体验。

深圳市南山博物馆馆长

Preface II

Italy is well known as the country with the most world cultural heritage sites. These sites date back to a long time ago and are of various types. The "Love, Luxury and Beauty in Classical Antiquity: Masterpieces from The Museo Archeologico Nazionale di Napoli", co-organized by Nanshan Museum and the MANN of Naples, is the third exhibition our museum has held that reflects Italian culture. This is another important exhibition with the aim of showcasing the world's great cultures.

Pompeii is located in the central west of Italy and is deeply influenced by ancient Greek and Roman cultures. The eruption of Mount Vesuvius over 1,900 years ago left this ancient city the way it was in 79 A.D., which allowed a large number of various cultural relics to be preserved. The exhibits in this exhibition are all from the MANN of Naples. We hope to reproduce the prosperous scene of Pompeii through these exquisite sculptures, pottery, murals, building components and other types of cultural relics, so that visitors can better understand the charming Italian culture.

In recent years, Nanshan Museum has held many high-quality exhibitions reflecting the cultural history of countries along the Belt and Road, which have been welcomed by visitors. In the future, we will continue to strengthen cultural exchanges and bring more exciting cultural experiences to the people in the Guangdong-Hong Kong-Macao Greater Bay Area.

Director of Nanshan Museum, Shenzhen

Qi Xin

目录

导言

第一单元 梦回盛世

第二单元 古希腊罗马时期的爱情神话

第三单元 快意人生：古罗马人对美好生活的热爱

第四单元 古代艺术中美的概念

第五单元 庞贝古城的再现

CONTENTS

古希腊罗马时期的爱情、奢华与美：
一点反思

古希腊和古罗马文明对西方世界的文化发展起到了决定性的作用，其影响深深地渗透在西方的历史、思想和思维方式中。

这一宝贵遗产有许多重要的组成部分，如古希腊与古罗马人精致的生活方式，即通过奢华的感官和认知手段充分欣赏生活的全部。这种奢华并非简单地炫耀财富或幸福，而是携有升华人们思想的正向意义，将寻找美作为一种生活方式，引导人类追求永恒的完美理想。

对此进行审视的那一刻，即是对古典思想进行反思的重要时刻。

从该角度出发，本展览旨在探讨古希腊和古罗马文明中的爱情、奢华和美的概念，以便中国观众了解西方文明基本价值观，理解与自身、与他人和谐相处的"美好生活"文化。

爱情

在古希腊罗马时期，提到"爱情"，人们首先想起的即是"爱神"。古希腊人称其为厄洛斯，古罗马人称之为丘比特。爱神这一力量的化身，在当时的文化和思想体系中占据着中心地位，以各自不同的形象产生着同样深刻的影响。

厄洛斯或丘比特的形象是带有武器的少年的神，其弓弦上经常射出致命的箭矢。受其影响的人则将无路可逃，坠入爱河。但爱不仅仅代表爱的感情，更代表强烈的欲望。情感和欲望是爱情的两面，但在古希腊罗马时期，它们则作为人类体验的两个独立时刻而被看待。例如在婚姻中，爱欲的存在只是为了让结合达到生育婚生子女的目的；感官之爱或激情之爱反而在婚姻之外的不同关系中得到体验。还有一件事能够恰好证明这一点，那就是：厄洛斯本身就生于阿佛洛狄忒的婚外恋情。阿佛洛狄忒是爱与美的象征，她完美结合了凡人的弱点与天堂的完美。

爱神是不遵循规则的。这并不是说这些规则对凡人不存在。相反，它们存在着，并且极为严格。如果只讨论女性性行为方面，就可以举出如下的例子：未婚女性必须严格遵守贞操；已婚女性必须同样严格地保有忠诚。但爱神并不重视规则，而是同样地在凡人、神灵、半人、动物、男人和女人之间创造出爱，因为爱神代表着一种神圣的力量，它没有限制，也没有人能抵抗它的进攻。

在古希腊文化中，爱情体验是受到阿佛洛狄忒保护的。阿佛洛狄忒女神主掌快乐与性的结合，是位出色的诱惑者。这位非常强大的女神被赋予了以快乐的方式改变世界的力量。阿佛洛狄忒诞生于大海的纯白泡沫中，许多对她的形容都与海洋有关，许多港口和海域都对她怀有深深的崇拜。爱与快乐的女神阿佛洛狄忒能够安抚自然万物，因此水手们向她寻求保护。由此也诞生了她赤裸身体的、美丽而闪亮的诗意形象，深远地影响着古代和现代艺术传统。

无论是在婚姻领域还是在自由关系中，所有的女性都会因为爱情和性的问题向阿佛洛狄忒求助。通常来说，少女们会向阿佛洛狄忒祈祷赐予她们丈夫或感谢她让自己得偿所愿，并供奉给她衣物、珠宝和装饰品。

阿佛洛狄忒是伟大爱情的主角，她是跛脚的火神与锻造之神赫菲斯托斯的妻子，她的情人是迷人而又凶猛残酷的战神阿瑞斯。阿佛洛狄忒与美少年阿多尼斯——这位无法抗拒的诱惑者——也有过火热的爱情。他们的关系激起了阿瑞斯的愤怒，阿瑞斯在一次狩猎旅行中放出一头野猪来攻击阿多尼斯，使他伤重而亡。阿佛洛狄忒与战神阿瑞斯爱抚和拥抱的形象，经常被厄洛斯们环绕着。厄洛斯们将神的可怕武器变成天真的游戏，不再只呈现爱情本身享有特权和挑衅的形象，而更强调阿佛洛狄忒的强大力量——她用温柔但非常坚固的美和爱的关系约束着战争和死亡。

奢侈及生活之乐

狄俄尼索斯是古希腊与古罗马文化所设想的最迷人、最复杂的神。其复杂性源于其多面性和难以捉摸但始终存在的特性。这一特征的基础是这位神的"差异性"，即他具有取消对立面的能力。事实上，狄俄尼索斯将男性与女性、疯狂与智慧、原始与文明结合在一起。狄俄尼索斯赐予人类葡萄树，葡萄串酿成的葡萄酒是古希腊和古罗马的顶级饮品，但它的反面则是带有破坏性的醉酒。

最能体现狄俄尼索斯力量的是戏剧，这是为纪念他而庆祝的节日中不可或缺的一部分。此外，狄俄尼索斯还体现着以阳具为象征存在的生命维度。同时，死亡也属他掌管，甚至在神话故事中，他还经历了重生。

狄俄尼索斯的新娘是克里特岛的公主阿里阿德涅，狄俄尼索斯始终忠于她。雅典英雄忒修斯战胜牛头人身怪后，将阿里阿德涅遗弃在纳克索斯岛，而狄俄尼索斯正是在此时遇见了阿里阿德涅。许多画像都描绘了狄俄尼索斯和妻子阿里阿德涅之间充满爱意和幸福的婚姻，他们身处众多萨提尔和迈那得斯们之间。狄俄尼索斯手中通常捏着的酒杯明确表现着葡萄酒这一标志性元素。由葡萄酒生出的醉意，结合着舞蹈和音乐，带来幸福、爱和狂喜。

长期以来，古罗马人用餐的地方相当简朴，家具也仅限于必需品。然而，在公元前 3 世纪和公元前 2 世纪之间，富裕的罗马家庭的住宅不断扩大，越来越多的空间用于会客和起居。在具有纪念意义的房屋中，卧躺餐厅尤为重要。那里，人们躺在欢宴床上用餐。这些床以马蹄形布置在桌子周围，铺放着舒适的垫子和毯子，人们可以舒适地躺在上面，将上半身靠在左边。

在会客厅里，富裕的家庭可以接待客人并放松身心。客厅四周布置着奢华而贵重的物品，人们普遍用较大的雕像、挂毯、壁画和马赛克来装饰环境。这些房间还配有桌子、长凳、烛台、火炉和火盆。为了强调奢华和放松的气氛，奴隶们在油灯中加入香精，用异国情调的气味取悦食客。

最富裕家庭的生活方式处处透露着奢侈，它不仅体现在拥有或展示的个人物品中，如珠宝首饰、精美面料和香水等，也在宴会等"特殊场合"中得到展现和强调。宴会是社交和政治互动的重要场合，巩固着亲属关系、从属关系或对主人的依赖关系。

古罗马的宴会是知识分子的社交场合，音乐和表演为宴会带来欢乐的气氛。食物也不再仅限于食用价值，而更是成为展示优雅和奢华的手段，代表着个人的社会地位。食物与美酒、音乐、歌唱、交谈和游戏一起，放大着快乐，营造出享受和炫耀的氛围。宴会令人联想到奢华，因而往往成为其代名词。人们通过展示一系列身份象征，提高自己在他人眼中的社会地位。

从维苏威火山地区壁画常描绘的欢乐场景中，我们能够感受到庞贝式的宴会的生动氛围。用小画装饰卧躺餐厅墙面的习俗和用途和今天并无不同。这些画详细描绘着周围环境的所有细节：欢宴床上覆盖着珍贵布料制成的靠垫和毯子、觥筹交错间闪闪发光的青铜瓶和银瓶、环绕着宴会客人的餐桌……宴会厅前的客厅中常装饰着描绘戏剧场景的小画，似乎为我们暗示着当时穿插于宴会中的精彩表演。静物主题的小画中则关注烹饪的美食和大地作物的美味，画中反复描绘着鱼、野味、蔬菜和水果。

古罗马人餐桌上使用的器具是由多种多样的材料制成的：从最不起眼的陶土，到玻璃，再到最珍贵的青铜和银，它们都见证着主人不同层次的财富水平。最常见的陶器是用细黏土制成的，即所谓的细陶。从公元 1 世纪初的奥古斯都时代开始，在意大利和罗马帝国的其他地区（如高卢）生产一种更精致的带有鲜红釉的陶器（红精陶）。当时广泛使用的还有透明薄玻璃制成的容器（水罐、高脚杯和玻璃杯），它们是静物画常常描绘的物品。餐桌用具包括用于盛放固体食物的容器和盛装、倾倒或饮用液体的容器。

食物放在大盘子里，每位用餐者使用较小的容器（例如不同形状的杯子和碗）来盛装自己食用的部分。当时人们用餐时主要使用汤匙，它是喝汤必备的，而餐叉的使用则未经证实。大量的文献也记载了用于盛装液体（水和酒）的各种容器，它们主要由青铜或玻璃制成，只有少数情况下是用银制成的。

葡萄酒用具包括双耳细颈瓶、双柄大口酒罐、用来混合酒（当时的酒是要经过调配才喝的）和舀酒的勺子、用来倒酒的酒罐、用来喝酒的高脚杯和玻璃杯、用来过滤酒的过滤器。具有古希腊风格的形状优雅的器皿，即所谓的茶炊，冬天可用来加热水，夏天则可以填加雪，并将雪压实，用以冷却葡萄酒。

花园是古罗马房屋中最重要的空间之一。它诞生于古罗马共和时代，最开始的主要功能是家庭菜园。随着时间的推移，古罗马上层阶级受古希腊文化影响，逐步肯定了古希腊人的生活方式，花园也经历了多次变革。公元前 2 世纪，在彻底征服古希腊之后，花园的概念发生了变化。一方面，引入了花卉栽培；另一方面，从严格的建筑角度来看，则引入了柱廊（带柱廊的花园）。古罗马人在花园度过一天的大部分时间。天气好的时候，他们喜欢到户外散步或在树荫下休息、阅读、写诗、讨论哲学或政治。

花园通常是精心打理的，里面有着令人印象深刻的建筑和装饰元素（雕塑、小的许愿龛、喷泉、水池、运河或光滑水面）。花园也是自我表现的重要媒介，是展示文化和财富的理想之地，也是精心设计的、展示艺术品收藏的场所，使人们在家中任何角度都能看见展示的艺术品。此外，花园还发挥至关重要的实用功能，在拥挤和混乱的城市环境中提供良好的光源和新鲜的空气，而鲜花和芳香植物的气味能掩盖外面传来的持久的、令人不快的气味。花园的装饰通常受到神话和戏剧的启发，尤其受到酒神游行文化的启发。酒神狄俄尼索斯在古希腊文化中象征着奢华、富裕、原始自然和户外生活的乐趣。

美

在历史的长河中，围绕美的观念，人类发展出了许多概念。在古代美学中就有和谐、对称、韵律、协调等。比起审美，它们更与道德相关。古希腊人将美的概念与优雅和尺度，尤其是和比例的概念联系在一起。当身体的所有部分达到平衡、对称和和谐时，身体就是美丽的。

在古希腊人看来，美是形状的完美比例，也是内在和谐的反映。理想的古希腊男人是英俊而有美德的。裸体是英雄的标志，是身心俱佳的象征。作为和谐的美表达着一个人的道德层面。一切吸引和引起我们钦佩其辉煌的事物，值得最高的尊重。美也表达着一个人的谦逊和平衡，即睿智。从这个角度来看，艺术和建筑作品也深受启发，通过各部分清晰和精确的比例追求对称和完美。

特洛伊国王普里阿摩斯在"白臂海伦"出现时低语道："貌似天仙"(《伊利亚特》，III 158)。当海伦这位真正的美人闯入战场，年迈的国王面对如此惊人的美，只能说"难怪，为了她，特洛伊人和胫甲坚固的阿开亚人经年奋战——谁能责备他们呢？"(《伊利亚特》，III 156–7)。

海伦是勒达和宙斯的女儿，因为半神的身份而美丽，更被认为是"世间最美丽的女人"。她代表着卓越的理想女性形象。美是一种神赐的礼物，它使人与神相似，但同时，它本身也具有很大的宿命性，可以显露出不幸的底色。事实上确实如此，海伦的命运就是以帕里斯的评判为标志的。这位年轻的牧羊人在一场女性的比赛中被选为裁判，以决定赫拉、雅典娜和阿佛洛狄忒中谁是最美丽的女神。三位女神争相承诺，将用"礼物"回报帕里斯。牧羊人最终接受了阿佛洛狄忒的礼物，因为阿佛洛狄忒曾答应他会娶到世界上最美丽的女人海伦。而海伦也的确与帕里斯偷情，由此引发了特洛伊战争。

海伦对男人的魅惑力是巨大的。同样令人印象深刻的是，她给这个世界带来无数死亡与毁灭，用自己的魅惑颠倒了众生的命运。正如我们所见，神赐的美丽同时带有积极和消极的意义。

维苏威火山地区的城市得以将最多的古代壁画装饰留存给今天的人们。这些壁画中有许多女性角色：女神、女英雄、女祭司、仆人和飞翔的形象。有时她们是刻板的人物，而有时她们的形象则带着明确的现实意味以及与日常生活的联系。

像在今天一样，即使在古罗马时期，女性的发型设计方式也千差万别。除了时尚的流行趋势外，这种多样性也来源于实践，因为特定的面相需要找到最合适的发型。不可否认，发型能赋予人很大一部分美感。然而，在古罗马文明的最早时期，一直到公元前1世纪，男性和女性的发型都非常简单：男性的短发往前梳；女性的头发用丝带向后扎或编成辫子，于颈背处打结。中分发型也很流行，波浪形的头发垂挂在前额和脖颈。

从公元前1世纪末开始，在屋大维娅(奥古斯都皇帝的妹妹)的简单发型之后，引领时尚的帝国公主们的发型变得越来越复杂。在朱里亚–克劳狄王朝(公元1世纪上半叶)，十分常见的是，宽大的波浪发从前额开始，在颈背上聚集成一个短马尾，或中分发型的波浪发垂至耳朵处。更精致的发型则是将头发聚成两大团卷发，遮住脸颊和耳朵的一部分。弗拉维王朝间(公元1世纪末)，女性将头发设计成非常复杂的卷发。公元2世纪开始，她们则广泛使用假发和发套。

书面和考古资料为我们提供了大量有关个人护理和女性化妆习俗的信息。古代的作家根据优劣将当时的化妆品进行区分。优质化妆品的药性保持身体的自然；劣质化妆品则提供人造的美感。化妆艺术从古埃及传到古希腊，再传到古意大利和古罗马，几经起伏，几个世纪以来一直被认为是骗人的技法。人们经常过度使用香水和香膏的行为导致坚决反对者的谴责，从而推动国家制定具体的相关法律。

从公元前 2 世纪末开始，奢侈品、珠宝首饰、贵重布料、宝石、香水、香精和东方香膏在古罗马大规模传播开来。这些奢侈品通过位于地中海贸易中心的大港口波佐利、古罗马在叙利亚以及亚历山大港的行省，广泛分布到了整个西地中海。

古罗马人通过面膜和香膏等化妆品来护理皮肤，它们的材质非常接近药剂。也有化妆品以罐装粉末的形式销售，供人们取所需数量调和使用。扇贝的壳也可以成为一种特殊的化妆品容器，粉末状物质或软膏被放置在一侧的贝壳中，另一侧的贝壳则像盖子一样起到封闭作用。这些化妆品通过丝绸之路从东方到达罗马。来自中亚的商队在亚历山大港汇合，从印度经波斯湾和红海的海上商队也以这个埃及港口为终点。从这里出发，珍贵的产品装在小巧优雅的香盒中运抵意大利。

香水有着古老的历史，最初来源于沐浴后使用的精油。古罗马作家普林尼将其发明归功于波斯人，不过在那之前，它已经在法老统治下的埃及使用了。它从花朵的花瓣或根、地中海灌木丛中的典型植物、香料或水果中提取，是精英阶层财富的体现，具有异常强大的诱惑力。

古埃及人是香水的大生产商和出口商。在古罗马时期，坎帕尼亚（意大利半岛南部）也兴起了很多香水生产中心，主要分布在卡普阿和那不勒斯，但经证实，在维苏威火山区也有适于制作香水的植物香精生产。香水被保存在埃及产的一整块雪花石膏制成的典型细长罐中，以防止香精变质，但雪花石膏价格十分昂贵，因此香水也被保存在其他形状的陶土容器中。从公元前 1 世纪末开始，人们开始广泛生产各种形状、大小和颜色的吹制玻璃香水罐。

香水在使用时可以直接用手指蘸取或适量倒出，一滴也不浪费。非常独特的是鸽子形的吹制玻璃香水罐，一旦装满，就用火焰密封。有需要时可以折断"鸽子"的喙或尾巴尖，倒出里面的香水。个人护理首先包括身体卫生，古罗马人通常使用公共浴场每天清洗身体。为了使皮肤恢复柔软，必须涂抹香膏和香油。

古罗马人不使用玻璃镜子，而是使用金属镜子。镜子的材料为青铜或银，形状或圆或方，配有手柄，可握在手中或挂在墙上。梳子和骨质或象牙的发簪则用于护理头发和为头发造型。特别的是，梳子很小，而且有两排密密的齿。有时梳子以凹面雕刻或浮雕装饰元素进行点缀。固定更复杂的发型时普遍会用到发簪，发簪的末端通常装饰有立体的形象。

策展人

玛丽亚露西娅 · 贾科

Love, luxury and beauty in the classical world: a reflection

The Greek and Roman civilizations played a decisive role in the development of the culture of the Western world, deeply permeating its history, ideas and way of thinking.

Among the most important aspects of this precious inheritance is undoubtedly the sophisticated way of understanding life by fully appreciating all its aspects through the sensory and cognitive tools belonging to the *luxus*, understood not as a mere ostentation of wealth or well-being, but as a way of life marked by the pursuit of beauty. A positive value that exalts the human mind because it leads it to strive for an ideal of perfection, beauty and eternity.

Questioning these aspects represents an important moment of reflection on classical thought. With this in mind, the exhibition, which aims to investigate the concepts of love, luxury and beauty in the Greek and Roman world, is an important contribution to the popularization of the founding values of Western civilization and to the dissemination and promotion of a "culture of living well" in harmony with oneself and others.

Love

In the Greek and Roman world, love was first and foremost a god, called Eros by the Greeks, and Cupid by the Romans. He was the embodiment of the power of love, a reflection of his central position in a culture and system of thought deeply marked by love in all its many shades.

Eros/Cupid was represented as an armed child-god who shot arrows with his bow. Those struck by it had no chance: they fell in love. But Cupid did not only personify the feeling of love, but also passionate desire. These were the two faces of love, feeling and desire, which, however, were experienced in classical antiquity as two separate moments of human experience. In marriage, for example, Eros was present only to enable the union to achieve its purpose, namely, the procreation of legitimate children. By contrast, the love of the senses or passionate love was experienced in different relationships outside of marriage as, moreover, evidenced by the very origins of Eros born, not coincidentally, out of an extramarital affair of Aphrodite, the goddess symbolic of beauty and love, who united the weaknesses of mortals with heavenly perfection.

Eros knew no rules but for mortals they existed and were very strict: for example, unmarried women were required to have strict chastity, and married women were required to have strict fidelity. But Eros did not care about rules and made love arise, indifferently, between mortal beings, gods, semi-human figures, animals, men and women. As a divine force, Eros had no limits and no one was able to resist his attacks.

The experience of love in Greek and Roman culture is placed under the auspices of Aphrodite, the goddess who is responsible for the sphere of pleasure and sexual union: she is the seductress par excellence.

Aphrodite is a most powerful goddess, endowed with a power capable of joyfully transforming the world. She is born from the white foam of the sea and many epithets link her to the marine element, just as there are numerous cults rendered to her in ports and seas: Aphrodite, goddess of eros and pleasure, pacifies the elements and therefore sailors sought her protection. She is born, therefore, beautiful and resplendent, naked from the sea, a poetic image that will fascinate ancient and modern artistic tradition.

All women turn to Aphrodite for what pertains to the love and sexual sphere, whether in the marital sphere or in free relationships: these are often maidens who pray to Aphrodite to grant them a husband or to thank her for obtaining one by giving her clothing, jewellery and ornaments.

Aphrodite is the protagonist of great loves: wife of Hephaestus, the cripple god of fire and metallurgy, she had as her lover the handsome Ares, fierce and cruel god of war. A passionate love was also that for Adonis, handsome and irresistible seducer: their relationship aroused the wrath of Ares, who during a hunting party unleashed a boar at the young man, mortally wounding him. The caresses and embraces between Aphrodite and Ares, god of war, often surrounded by heroes who transform the god's fearsome weapons into innocent playthings, far from representing exclusively the privileged and provocative image of the physicality of love, emphasize above all the power and strength of the goddess, who enchains with sweet but very strong laces of beauty and love the instruments of war and death.

Luxury and joy of life

Dionysus is the most fascinating and complex god that Greek-Roman culture has conceived; a complexity that stems from his being multifaceted, elusive but constantly present. Underlying this characteristic is his ability to undo opposites. Dionysus, in fact, combines male and female, madness and wisdom, savage and civilized. He is the god who gives men the vine, from whose bunches wine is made, the drink par excellence of the Greek-Roman world, but which has its reverse in destructive drunkenness.

The most obvious manifestation of the power of Dionysus is the theatre, an integral part of the festivals celebrated in his honour. Dionysus, moreover, embodies the vital dimension of existence, symbolized by the phallus, and at the same time the sphere of death is also his own, experiencing, in the mythical tale, rebirth as well.

His bride is the Cretan princess Ariadne to whom he remains ever faithful, whom he collects in Naxos where she had been abandoned by the Athenian hero Theseus on his return from his victorious expedition on the Minotaur. There are numerous images that portray him next to his bride Ariadne in a loving and joyous union between satyrs and maenads: wine, which he clasps in his hands, remains his defining element, the instrument of intoxication that leads to happiness, love and ecstasy achieved through dancing and music.

For a long time, the place where ancient Romans ate meals had been rather austere with furniture limited to the essentials. However, between the 3rd and 2nd centuries BC, the dwellings of wealthy Roman families expanded, and more and more space was allocated to spaces of representation and living rooms. In monumental houses, special importance is given to the dining room, the triclinium, where people ate while lying on *klinai* (convivial beds) arranged in a horseshoe shape around a table. They were made comfortable by pillows and blankets, on which one could lie comfortably, resting on one's left side.

In the spaces of representation, reception rooms, wealthy families could receive guests and relax, surrounded by luxurious and valuable objects. It was the tendency to decorate the room by embellishing it with statues, wall hangings, frescoes and mosaics, often of large dimensions. These rooms were also furnished with tables, stools, candelabra, stoves and braziers. To increase the atmosphere of luxury and relaxation, slaves added scented essences to oil lamps, delighting diners with exotic scents.

In more affluent homes, luxury found expression in the modus vivendi and invested the personal items owned or displayed: jewellery, fine fabrics, perfumes. Luxury also finds its manifestation and exaltation in "special occasions", such as banquets. These were important occasions of social and political interaction, during which ties of kinship, affiliation or dependence on the master of the house were consolidated.

The Roman banquet is a social and intellectual gathering, enlivened by music and entertainment, during which food becomes the pretext for exhibiting refinement and luxury, as manifestations of one's social status. Food, accompanied by wine and music, singing, conversation, and games, becomes an exaltation of pleasures, an occasion for enjoyment and ostentation. The banquet is associated with pomp and often becomes a simulation of luxury, through a set of status symbols exhibited, with the purpose of elevating one's social status in the eyes of others.

The atmosphere of the Pompeian banquets is still alive in the frequent scenes found in the Vesuvian paintings. Small paintings that decorated the walls of triclinia seem not to deviate from contemporary habits and customs. They depict all the details of the surroundings: pillows and blankets in fine fabrics covering the beds, the bronze and silver vases glittering among the toasts of the banqueters, the tables surrounded by the banqueters. Often in the rooms preceding the banquet room, small paintings appear with theatrical scenes, which seem to allude to the performances that were held during the banquets. In the still life paintings, attention to the delicacies of the kitchen and the taste of the products of the earth appear: depictions of fish, game, vegetables and fruit are recurrent.

The pottery used on the tables of the ancient Romans was made of the most diverse materials: from the humblest clay, to glass, to the most valuable bronze and silver, testifying to the different levels of wealth of the owner. The most common pottery was made of fine clay, the so-called fine pottery. From the beginning of the 1st century AD, in the Augustan age, more refined bright red glazed pottery (terra sigillata) became widespread, produced both in Italy and in other regions of the Empire, such as Gaul. Also in common use were containers (pitchers, cups, glasses) made of thin transparent glass, often reproduced in still life paintings.

Table service consisted of vessels intended for solid foods and those for holding, pouring, or drinking liquids. Food was presented in large serving dishes, from which each diner served themselves using smaller containers, such as cups and small bowls. The only cutlery was the spoon, while the use of a fork is not attested. Widely documented are the various containers intended for liquids, water and wine, made mostly of bronze or glass and only exceptionally of silver.

Wine service included amphorae, craters for wine, ladles for mixing (wine was not drunk pure) and drawing it, pitchers for pouring it, cups and glasses for drinking, and strainers for filtering it. Elegantly shaped vessels of Hellenistic derivation, the so-called samovars, were used in winter to heat water, while in summer wine could be cooled with snow pressed into special strainers.

Also the garden was one of the most important rooms in the Roman home. It arose in the Republican age with the predominant function of a domestic vegetable garden, and over time, it underwent numerous transformations as a "Greek-style" lifestyle became established, following the reception of Hellenistic culture by the Roman upper class. In the 2nd century BC, after the final conquest of Greece, the very idea of the garden was transformed with the introduction, on the one hand, of the cultivation of flowers and, on the other hand, from a strictly architectural point of view, with the introduction of the peristyle (porticoed garden). In the garden the Romans spent a good part of the day. In fine weather they loved to stroll in the open air or relax in the shade of a tree to read, write poetry, discuss philosophy or politics.

Gardens, usually well-kept and laid out with impressive architectural and decorative elements (sculptures, small votive shrines, fountains, ponds, canals or artificial pools of water), were also an important means of self-representation, ideal places to show the world one's culture and wealth or to display a collection of artworks according to a precise figurative program that made them visible from anywhere in the house. They also served a critically important practical function, providing, in crowded and chaotic urban settings, a good source of light and fresh air, while the scent of flowers and aromatic plants covered and made any lingering and unpleasant odours from outside more tolerable. Their decoration was usually inspired by mythical and theatrical themes but especially by the Dionysian world to celebrate Dionysus as the god of Hellenistic *tryphè* (luxury, pageantry), wild nature, and the joy of the outdoors.

Beauty

Throughout history man has developed many ideas around the idea of beauty: in ancient aesthetics we speak of harmony, symmetry, and eurythmy to which ethical rather than aesthetic virtues are associated. With the idea of beauty the ancient Greeks associated the concepts of grace, measure and above all proportion: a body is beautiful when there is balance, symmetry and harmony among all its parts.

In the Greek vision, beauty is the perfect proportion of forms but also a reflection of inner harmony. The ideal Greek man is beautiful and virtuous. The naked body is the distinctive mark of the hero, a symbol of physical and moral excellence. Beauty expresses the moral dimension of a man: anything that attracts and arouses our admiration for its splendour is also worthy of the highest esteem. Being beautiful also expresses a man's ability to be moderate and balanced, in other words, wise. With this in mind, artistic and architectural productions were also inspired by the quest for symmetry and perfection achieved through clear and precise proportions of individual parts.

"Wondrously like is she to the immortal goddesses" (Iliad, III 158). These are the words almost whispered by Priam, king of Troy, upon the appearance of "Helen with the white arms," true beauty personified, who bursts into the theatre of war. The elderly king, in the presence of such beauty, can do nothing but note that "neither the Trojans nor the Achaeans are to blame for the pains endured during the war because of such a woman" (Iliad, III 156-7).

Daughter of Leda and Zeus, beautiful by semi-divine nature but also considered "the most beautiful of all women," she embodies the feminine ideal par excellence. Beauty is a gift of divine origin, making men similar to the gods, but at the same time, possessing within itself a good dose of fatality that can prove to bring misfortune. Indeed, Helen's fate is marked by the events that follow the judgment of Paris, the young shepherd chosen to decide which of Hera, Athena, and Aphrodite is the most beautiful. The three goddesses compete by promising their "gifts" to Paris. He accepts the gift of Aphrodite, who had promised him in marriage the most beautiful woman in the world, Helen, who becomes an adulteress against her will and the trigger for the Trojan War.

The fascination exercised by Helen on men was enormous, as was the mass of deaths, mourning and ruins that she brought to the world, upsetting the lives of men and women who had to suffer due to her seductive power. The gift of beauty, as we can see, is full of positive and negative meanings at the same time.

The Vesuvian cities have returned, due to their sudden destruction, the greatest amount of pictorial wall decorations that the ancient world could leave us. Female characters appear in many of them: goddesses, heroines, priestesses, servants, allegorical personifications and flying figurines, in a multifaceted representation of the female world. Sometimes they are stereotypical figures, but other times their depiction has a clear realistic intent and a connection to everyday life.

Just like nowadays, the way women's hair was styled in Roman times was extremely varied. Apart from the trends imposed by fashion, the variety practically stemmed from the need to find the most suitable hairstyle for a specific physiognomy. The hair is undeniably entrusted with a large part of an individual's beauty; however, in the earliest period of Rome's civilization and up to the 1st century BC, hairstyles, both male and female, were extremely simple. Short locks raked forward for men, hair gathered in a knot at the nape of the neck, held back by ribbons or gathered in braids for women. A hairstyle with central parting, with hair flowing wavy down the forehead and neck, is also in vogue.

From the end of the 1st century BC, after the simple hairstyle adopted by Octavia (sister of Emperor Augustus), the hairstyles of imperial princesses, who dictated fashion, would become increasingly complex. In the Julio-Claudian era (first half of the 1st century AD) wide wavy hairstyles are very common, starting from the forehead and gathering in a short ponytail at the nape of the neck, those with a central parting from which wavy locks detach toward the ears, and those, more elaborate in which the hair is gathered in two large masses of curls, covering part of the cheeks and ears, are very common. In the Flavian era (late 1st century AD) women had their hair styled in complicated curls, leading up to the adoption of hairpieces and wigs widely in use from the 2nd century AD onward.

Written and archaeological sources inform us abundantly about uses related to personal care and female grooming. Ancient authors distinguished between good cosmetics, that is, the part of medicine aimed at preserving the body its naturalness, from bad cosmetics, which procures an artificial beauty. The art of cosmetics, which from the Egyptian world was transmitted to the Greeks and from there to the Italic and Roman worlds, was, in alternating times, considered over the centuries to be the art of deception: the often immoderate use of perfumes and ointments led the fierce opponents to condemn their use, prompting the enactment of special laws.

From the end of the 2nd century BC onwards, the Roman world witnessed a gradual spread of unbridled luxury, jewellery, fabrics and precious stones, perfumes, essences and oriental ointments. Through Pozzuoli, the great port at the centre of trade in the Mediterranean and home to Syrian and Alexandrian colonies, the objects of *luxuria* spread throughout the western Mediterranean.

Cosmetics dealt with skin care through masks and ointments and were very close to pharmacopoeia. There were also makeup products, usually marketed in the form of powders contained in jars, to be taken in the desired amount and mixed. A special type of cosmetic vessel consisted of shells of the genus *pecten*, where the powdered substance or ointment was placed in one valve and covered with the other. These products reached Rome from the East via the Silk Road: caravan ships from Central Asia converged in Alexandria, as did the sea routes from India via the Persian Gulf and the Red Sea, which had their terminal in the Egyptian port. From here, the precious products arrived in Italy in small, elegantly crafted perfume holders.

Originating as an addition to oils used after bathing, perfume has ancient origins. Pliny attributes its invention to the Persians but it was already in use in Pharaonic Egypt. An expression of the wealth of elites and a very powerful tool of seduction, perfumes in the ancient world were made from flowers (whose petals or roots were used), from plants typical of the Mediterranean, from spices or from fruits.

Great producers and exporters were the Egyptians although, in Roman times, production centres sprang up in the region of Campania itself: Capua and Naples were the main ones, but also in the Vesuvian area there are attested productions of plant essences suitable for perfume production. Perfumes were then stored in *alabastra*, typical elongated jars made in Egypt from a block of alabaster. They prevented the perfumed essence from deteriorating but were very expensive, therefore, they were joined by earthenware containers, also made in other forms. Beginning in the late 1st century BC, the production of blown-glass balsamarii jars of various shapes, sizes and colours became widespread.

Perfumed substances were drawn directly with the fingers or poured in modest amounts, without wasting a single drop. Very original are the dove-shaped blown-glass balsam jars that, once filled, were flame-sealed; if necessary, its beak or tail tip was broken off and its contents poured out. Personal care began with body hygiene: the rule was to wash every day, commonly using public baths. To restore softness to the skin, it was essential to apply ointments and scented oil.

The Romans did not use glass mirrors, but rather metal mirrors made of bronze or silver of round or square shape, equipped with a handle to be held in the hand or suspended from the wall, while combs and pins made of bone or ivory were used for hair care and styling. In particular, combs were small and with a double row of very dense teeth; sometimes they could be embellished with engraved or embossed decorative elements. To secure more complex hairstyles, the use of pins, the ends of which were often decorated, was quite common.

Curator of the exhibition

ML Grecco

盛世爱情

庞贝古城的传奇，源于一个"身死方成永恒"的凄美故事。被火山掩埋前的庞贝是一座深受古希腊古罗马文化影响的城市，经济发达，物产丰美，一片盛世景象。然而在短短的几个小时内，命运的岩浆滚滚而至，整个城市被彻底掩埋，一场繁华盛世也就此终结。

然而庞贝的魅力不止于此。18 世纪到 19 世纪，欧洲最伟大的知识分子们跨越意大利半岛，只为来到被火山掩埋的庞贝和赫库兰尼姆古城遗址接受古典文明的洗礼。欧洲知识分子与古典艺术的这场邂逅，对整个西方审美精神的发展起到重要作用，促使人们重新思考美的理念及其本质。庞贝古城所代表的，是古希腊、古罗马文明中一种更为恒久的理想：爱与美的理想。

审视爱与美的那一刻，便是对古典思想进行回溯的重要时刻。生命的痕迹也许会被时间抹去，然而爱的力量永生不灭。

这就是"盛世爱情"展览诞生的缘起。

本次展览与世界上最具盛名的考古博物馆之一——意大利那不勒斯国家考古博物馆再度合作，围绕爱与美的主题构建了一条观展路线，展品多数来自庞贝、赫库兰尼姆遗址和大希腊地区遗址。人类的悲剧和艺术的永恒性构成了这些文物的双重面貌，成为艺术家们汲取灵感的源泉。

展览从赫库兰尼姆古城的纸莎草别墅和庞贝古城的农牧神之家展开。之所以借助这两处神秘之地的力量，是因为这两地发掘出的文物能够展示出古罗马雕塑及其参考的古希腊雕像范例所达到的至高水准。

俯瞰大海的纸莎草别墅是古罗马时代的大型建筑，很可能属于路奇乌斯·皮索所有。他是著名的恺撒大帝的岳父，十分富有。自 18 世纪末以来，纸莎草别墅促进学者们的研究活动，激发艺术家和古代艺术爱好者们的想象力，成为考古发掘的神话。正是根据挖掘和模拟重建的成果，美国石油大亨让·保罗·盖蒂在加利福尼亚州的马里布市复建了这座大型住宅，目前作为博物馆使用。博物馆内收藏着庞贝古城发掘出的最完好的一部分雕像，包括经历维苏威火山喷发而毫发无损的青铜雕像。

展览中首先展出的"赫耳墨斯坐像"正是来自纸莎草别墅。作品表现的是这位众神使者、旅行之神和运动者保护神稍作休息及思考的瞬间。赫耳墨斯还被柏拉图视为话语的发明者，因而也是对话和交流的象征。因此，"赫耳墨斯坐像"作为首件作品开启本次展览。此外，1754 年在赫库兰尼姆古城出土了一组著名群雕，它们呈现着五位女舞者，更准确地说，是五位运水女子的形象。而纸莎草别墅发掘出的"5619 号女舞者"雕像，正是这组群雕五位女子中一位的复制品。曾被德国考古学家温克尔曼命名为"女舞者们"的五位动态女子群像，以自身简洁完美的形体，代表着一场永恒的、追寻美之源头的视觉之旅。

从古罗马一位重要地方法官的别墅——农牧神之家中，则出土了青铜像"起舞的农牧神"。展览中展出的是原件的珍贵复制品，原件保存在那不勒斯国家考古博物馆中不予外借。农牧神之家是庞贝古城的另一处标志性考古遗址，这里发掘出的著名作品"亚历山大马赛克"是古代最珍贵的马赛克作品之一。

"起舞的农牧神"呈现的是一位在古罗马文化中代表着自然、乡村和森林的小神。他赤身裸体、精瘦而又肌肉发达，似乎即将翩翩起舞。作品雕刻精美，极为自然地展现了人体自然状态下的运动、和谐与美感。

爱情，是古希腊罗马时期永恒的话题。先人将他们对爱情的痴迷与痛苦都注入了神话形象中。爱以多种形态呈现，展览的第二部分，呈现的就是不同形态的爱情神话。雕塑"伽倪墨得斯与鹰"中展现了古代理想中的绝世容颜：荷马称伽倪墨得斯为那个时代最俊美的凡人，连宙斯都爱上了他，不惜化身为鹰将他带去奥林匹斯山，让他成为众神的侍酒者。在此后千年的西方艺术中，伽倪墨得斯一直是艺术家们竞相表现的神话人物。

雕像"海中的阿佛洛狄忒"中的阿佛洛狄忒，是古希腊神话中掌管爱与美以及生育的女神。从古希腊文化崇拜的角度来看，有关她的神话是多种多样的。海中诞生的阿佛洛狄忒被尊为海洋生物的女神、水手的保护神。庞贝古城的众多壁画描绘着她从水中贝壳诞生的美丽景象。在这里，女神正以端庄的姿势沐浴。她稍稍俯身，双手和双臂遮住身体和胸部。女神的发型十分精致，头发在后脑勺和头顶各打了一个髻，展现出类似蝴蝶结的形态。

"波索斯雕像"呈现的则是触不可及的爱情。与厄洛斯和希莫勒斯一样同为爱神之子的波索斯，代表的是爱而不得时生出的苦恼与渴望。是遗憾，是留恋，是一种模糊的情绪，因为它同时暗示着因想要被爱而全身心投入的热情冲动，暗示着爱而不得的痛苦创伤、空虚和不可逾越的距离。

爱，不仅关乎激情，更是一种引导人们回归天性的强大力量。在接下来的第三单元中，爱演变为酒神所代表的生活的陶醉和疯狂，展现的是古罗马人对人间美好生活的热爱。酒神狄俄尼索斯代表着狂喜、热爱和欢乐，代表着人类身上无法控制的冲动和存在于生物的原始本能。此外，他还被认为是戏剧的始祖。酒神狄俄尼索斯对人们的生活方式产生了长远影响，本展览将展示美食与美酒带来的乐趣，并通过作为聚会欢宴场所的庞贝式住宅和花园，展示古罗马人对日常生活的热爱。

在这个部分之后，展览将转向探讨古代艺术中美的概念，以及爱和美的关联。特洛伊的绝代佳人海伦拥有半神的身份，她的倾城之色使得神和人之间产生了联系，也使得爱上她美丽容颜的人们颠倒了命运。本单元还将展示具象的美的概念，以及人们追求美的方式。

展览以一个沉浸式展厅作结。本展厅围绕一具庞贝年轻女子身体的石膏铸像而设，以第一人称讲述她在生命终结之前对爱与美的思考。维苏威火山喷发的瞬间，肉身消亡，生活的一切乐趣瞬间消殒，然而爱和美却将生命的形式化为永恒。

"盛世爱情"是一次因爱而起的旅程，诚邀观众朋友一同走进那个将爱视为绝对理想的时代。它是对神祇的虔诚奉献，也是对美不计代价的纯粹追求；它是拥有时的欢欣，也是触不可及时的惆怅；它是对神意的信仰，也是对生活的留恋；它既在天上，更在人间。

没有你，

哪怕我成了神，

也终将湮灭。

（庞贝，拉丁语铭文）

执行策展人

Flourishing Love

The legend of Pompeii originates from the poignant story that Pompeii "had to die to become eternal". Before it was buried by volcanic ash, Pompeii, deeply influenced by Greek and Roman culture, was a flourishing city of great beauty and economic development. However, in just a few hours, the magma of fate rolled in, the entire city was completely buried, and a prosperous era ended.

Nevertheless, the charm of Pompeii is more than this. From the eighteenth century to the nineteenth century, the greatest European intellectuals traversed the Italian peninsula just to reach the great archaeological areas of Pompeii and Herculaneum, buried due to volcanic eruption, and become spiritually immersed in the classical civilization. This encounter between European intellectuals and classical art played an important role in the development of the entire Western aesthetic spirit, prompting people to rethink the idea of beauty and its essence. What Pompeii represents is a more permanent ideal in Greco-Roman civilization: the ideal of love and beauty.

Questioning the aspects of love and beauty represents an important moment of reflection on classical thought. The traces of life may be erased by time, but the power of love never dies.

This is the origin of the exhibition *Love, Luxury and Beauty in Classical Antiquity*.

Cooperating again with one of the most prestigious archaeological museums in the world, the National Archaeological Museum of Naples, Italy, we have constructed a path based on the theme of love and beauty. Most of the artefacts come from the archaeological sites of Pompeii, Herculaneum and Magna Graecia. The human drama and the revealed eternity of art constitute the dual aspect of these cultural relics, and become the source from which artists drew inspiration.

The story begins with the Villa of the Papyri in Herculaneum and the House of the Faun in Pompeii. We use the power of these two mythical sites because from these places originate finds that show us the elevated level reached by Roman statuary and Greek reference models.

The Villa of the Papyri is a large architectural construction from the Roman period, overlooking the sea, owned by a very wealthy owner, Lucio Pisone, father-in-law of Julius Caesar, which has become a myth of archaeological excavations since the late eighteenth century, fuelling the activities of scholars and the imagination of artists and lovers of ancient art. It was from the results of the excavations and reconstructions that the American oilman Jean Paul Getty made a replica and turned it into a great mansion in Malibu, now a museum site, complete with all the statuary found that represents the best part of the Pompeian discoveries, including intact bronze statues that were not damaged by the eruption of Vesuvius.

From the Villa of the Papyri comes the Seated Hermes sculpture that begins our exhibition overview. The statue is depicted in a moment of rest and reflection. He is messenger of the gods, god of travel and protector of gymnasiums and considered by Plato the inventor of speech and therefore the symbol of dialogue and communication. Therefore, the first artwork introduces our tale. From the same villa comes a dancer, a copy from the famous group of five dancers, water bearers, found at Herculaneum in 1754. Referred to as "dancers" by Winckelmann, the five women in motion rise to the physiognomy of pure forms and volumes, coming to represent a timeless visual journey to discover the origin of beauty.

From the House of the Faun, an urban villa of an important Roman magistrate, instead comes the bronze faun, a copy of the immovable original preserved at the National Archaeological Museum in Naples. Another symbolic site of Pompeian archaeology where, among others, the famous mosaic of Alexander the Great in battle, one of the most valuable mosaics in all of antiquity, was found.

The dancing faun is a minor deity who represents, in the Roman world, the deity of nature, the countryside and the woods. He is a naked, lean, muscular man with feet that hint at a dance step. The execution of the work is refined and effective in naturally rendering the movement, harmony and beauty of the human body in its natural state.

Love, the eternal theme of classical times. The ancestors of ancient Greece and Rome infused mythological images with the obsession and pain that is born from love. Thus, love is represented in many different shapes. The second part of the exhibition, in fact, presents different types of myths about love. The sculpture Ganymede and the eagle portrays the perfect face in ancient ideals: Homer described him as the most beautiful of all mortals of his time, so beautiful that even Zeus fell in love with him and in the form of an eagle abducted him to take him to Olympus and make him the cupbearer of the gods. In the following millennium, Ganymede has always been a mythological character who had extraordinary success throughout the art of the Western painters.

Aphrodite from the sculpture Aphrodite Marina, is a goddess of love, beauty and the fertility in Greek myths. From the standpoint of Hellenic worship her myth was diversified; as Aphrodite Marina she was worshipped as a goddess of sea creatures protector of seafarers. Famous are the Pompeian frescoes depicting her rising from the water in a shell. In this artwork, Aphrodite is at the baths in the demure position. She in fact bends slightly over herself to cover her pubis and breasts with her hands and arms. Her hairstyle is rather peculiar, with her hair knotted both at the nape of her neck and on her head in the form of a bow.

Thus follows the statue of Pothos, the desire for love that melts the limbs. A son of Aphrodite like Eros and Himeros, Pothos represents desire toward absent love. It is regret, it is nostalgia. An ambiguous feeling, since it implies at the same time the passionate impulse of the whole being toward the fullness of the beloved presence and the painful trauma of absence, the realization of an emptiness, of an insurmountable distance.

Love is not just about passion, it is a greater force that leads people back to their primordial nature. In the third section of the exhibition the declension of beauty addresses the theme of intoxication of living and delirium embodied by the figure of Dionysus, showing the Roman love for a good life. Dionysus is a god who represents the mad, the lover and the ecstatic. The human energy that does not control impulses, the primordial and instinctual spark present in every living being. In addition, he is also considered inventor of the theatre. The long-lasting influence of Dionysus on people permeated their way of life, so this exhibition will showcase the pleasures of table and wine, and the love of the ancient Romans for the good life on earth, through the Pompeian domus and garden as a place of otium and convivial gatherings.

After this section, the exhibition turns to investigate the concept of beauty in ancient art and the association between love and beauty. Helen of Troy, a woman of matchless beauty, is of semi-divine nature. Her exeeding charm made a connection between gods and humans, upsetting the fates of people fallen for her beautiful appearance. This section will also demonstrate the concept of figurative beauty and the way people pursue it.

The exhibition closes with an immersive room built around a Pompeian cast of a female body, narrating in the first person her thoughts on love and beauty before the end of her life. The moment the volcano Vesuvius erupted, the body died, and all the joys of life disappeared instantly, yet love and beauty transformed the form of life into eternity.

Love, Luxury and Beauty in Antiquity is a journey started by love, and an invitation to visitors to walk into the era when love was regarded as an absolute ideal. Love is the devout dedication to the gods, and the pure pursuit of beauty regardless of the price; it is the joy of possession, and the melancholy of untouchability; it is the belief in the gods, and the nostalgia for life; it is in heaven, but also on earth.

PEREAM SINE TE SI DEVS ESSE VELIM

Let me perish without you if I should wish to be a god

Executive Curator

Qian Qian

导言
Introduction

古希腊罗马时期的爱情、奢华与美

古希腊和古罗马文明对西方世界的文化发展起到了关键性的作用，其影响深深地渗透在西方历史、思想和思维方式中。

在古希腊和古罗马文明的影响下，庞贝发展成了一座具有相当规模的城市。被火山灰掩埋前的庞贝，风景宜人，经济发达，物产丰美，城市文明发展到了令人惊叹的地步。

庞贝人发扬了古希腊与古罗马人精致的生活方式，他们极尽奢华之能事，用一切感官去享受生活的馈赠。这种奢华并非简单地炫耀财富或幸福，而是以寻找美、创造美作为生活方式，用爱去追求永恒的完美理想。

审视爱与美的那一刻，便是对古典思想进行回溯的重要时刻。

本展览旨在探讨古希腊和古罗马文明中的爱情、奢华和美的概念，邀请中国观众一同走进那个将爱和美视为理想的时代。生活的痕迹也许会被时间抹去，然而爱的力量永生不灭。

Love, Luxury and Beauty in Classical Antiquity

The Greek and Roman civilizations played a decisive role in the development of the culture of the Western world, deeply permeating its history, ideas and way of thinking.

Under the influence of ancient Greek and Roman civilizations, Pompeii developed into a city of considerable size. Before it was buried by volcanic ash, Pompeii was a city of great beauty, economic development and astonishing urban civilisation.

The people of Pompeii developed the refined lifestyle of the ancient Greeks and Romans, understanding life by fully appreciating all its aspects through the sensory and cognitive tools belonging to extreme luxury, which is not as a mere ostentation of wealth or well-being, but as a way of life marked by the pursuit and creation of beauty, an almost devout love for the ideal of eternal perfection.

Questioning these ideals of love and beauty is an important moment of reflection on classical thought. The exhibition aims to investigate the concepts of love, luxury and beauty in the Greco-Roman world, inviting visitors to step into a time when love and beauty were considered high ideals. The traces of life may be erased by time, but the power of love never dies.

公元前520年
520 BC

希腊红绘人物容器
日益盛行
Development of
the red-figure
vase painting in
Greece

公元前800年
800 BC

奥斯坎人在庞贝
建立大约5个定居点
The Oscans established
approximately 5
settlements in Pompeii

公元前304年
304 BC
第二次萨姆尼特战
庞贝以"盟友"身份
罗马同盟的一部分
End of the Second
Samnite War and
Pompeii becomes
part of Roman
confederation
as "ally"

约公元前423年
c. 423 BC

萨姆尼特人
开始统治庞贝
和赫库兰尼姆
Samnite rule over
Pompeii and
Herculaneum begins

公元前700-前500年
700 BC – 500 BC

伊特鲁里亚人争夺坎帕尼亚地区
Etruscans contest the region
of Campania

西周
公元前1046-前771年
Western Zhou Dynasty
1046 BC-771 BC

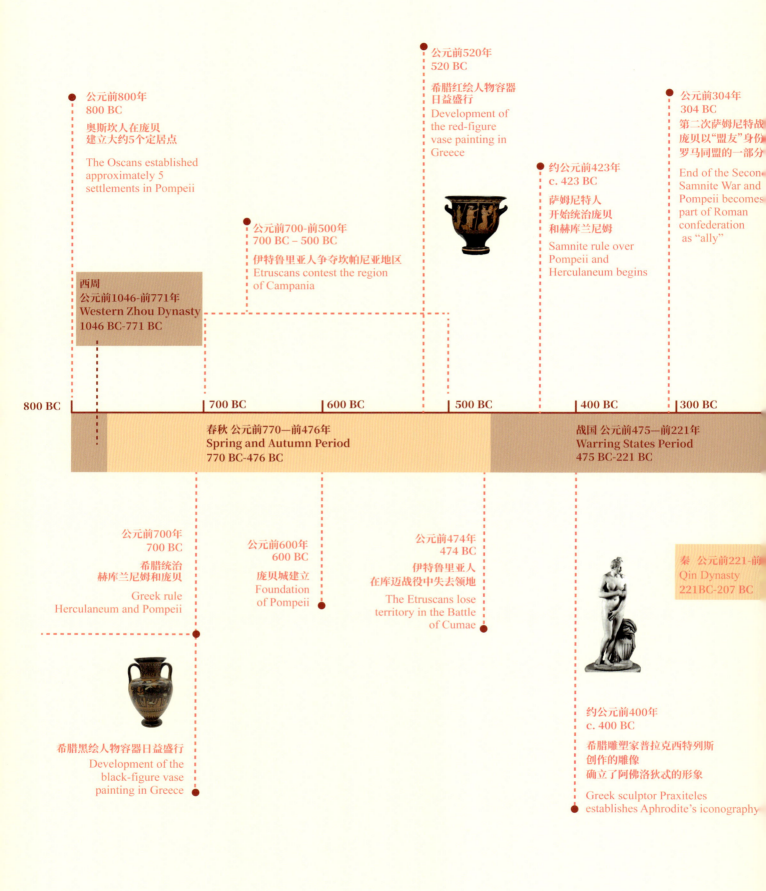

800 BC　　　700 BC　　　600 BC　　　500 BC　　　400 BC　　　300 BC

春秋 公元前770—前476年
Spring and Autumn Period
770 BC-476 BC

战国 公元前475—前221年
Warring States Period
475 BC-221 BC

公元前700年
700 BC

希腊统治
赫库兰尼姆和庞贝
Greek rule
Herculaneum and Pompeii

公元前600年
600 BC

庞贝城建立
Foundation
of Pompeii

公元前474年
474 BC

伊特鲁里亚人
在库迈战役中失去领地
The Etruscans lose
territory in the Battle
of Cumae

秦 公元前221-前
Qin Dynasty
221BC-207 BC

希腊黑绘人物容器日益盛行
Development of the
black-figure vase
painting in Greece

约公元前400年
c. 400 BC

希腊雕塑家普拉克西特列斯
创作的雕像
确立了阿佛洛狄忒的形象
Greek sculptor Praxiteles
establishes Aphrodite's iconography

约公元前180年
c. 180 BC

农牧神之家建成
House of the
Faun was built

公元前89年
89 BC

罗马将军
卢基乌斯·科尔
内利乌斯·苏拉
征服庞贝

Pompeii
conquered by
the Roman
general Lucius
Cornelius Sulla

公元前20-前10年
20 BC – 10 BC

庞贝第三风格壁画盛行, 直至公元79年
The Third Pompeian style of wall painting
was popular and was used until 79 AD

公元6年
62 AD

地震侵袭庞贝及赫库兰尼姆
Earthquake hits
Pompeii
and Herculaneum

1709年
1709 AD

赫库兰尼姆
古城被发现

Herculaneum
is discovered

1763年
1763 AD

发现包含庞贝城名称的铭文
"人民共有的庞贝"

Discovery of an epigraph
containing the name of the
city of Pompeii "Rei publicae
Pompeianorum"

BC	100 BC	0	100 AD	1700 AD	1800 AD

西汉 公元前202—公元25年
Western Han Dynasty
202 BC-25 AD

东汉 公元25—220年
Eastern Han Dynasty
25 AD-220 AD

......

清 公元1644—1911年
Qing Dynasty
1644 AD-1911 AD

公元前91年
91 BC

反抗罗马统治的起义
"同盟者战争"爆发

Revolt against Rome
during the Social War

公元79年
79 AD

维苏威火山爆发

Eruption of
Mount Vesuvius

1748年
1748 AD

庞贝古城的发现和挖掘工作开始

Discovery of Pompeii and
excavations begin

元前200年
0 BC

贝第一风格
画开始盛行

st
mpeian
le of wall
sco
veloped

公元前60-前50年
60 BC – 50 BC

纸莎草
别墅建成

The Villa of the
Papyri was built

公元50-100年
50 AD– 100 AD

弗拉维王朝式样
的发型盛行

Flavian Dynasty hairstyles
were popular

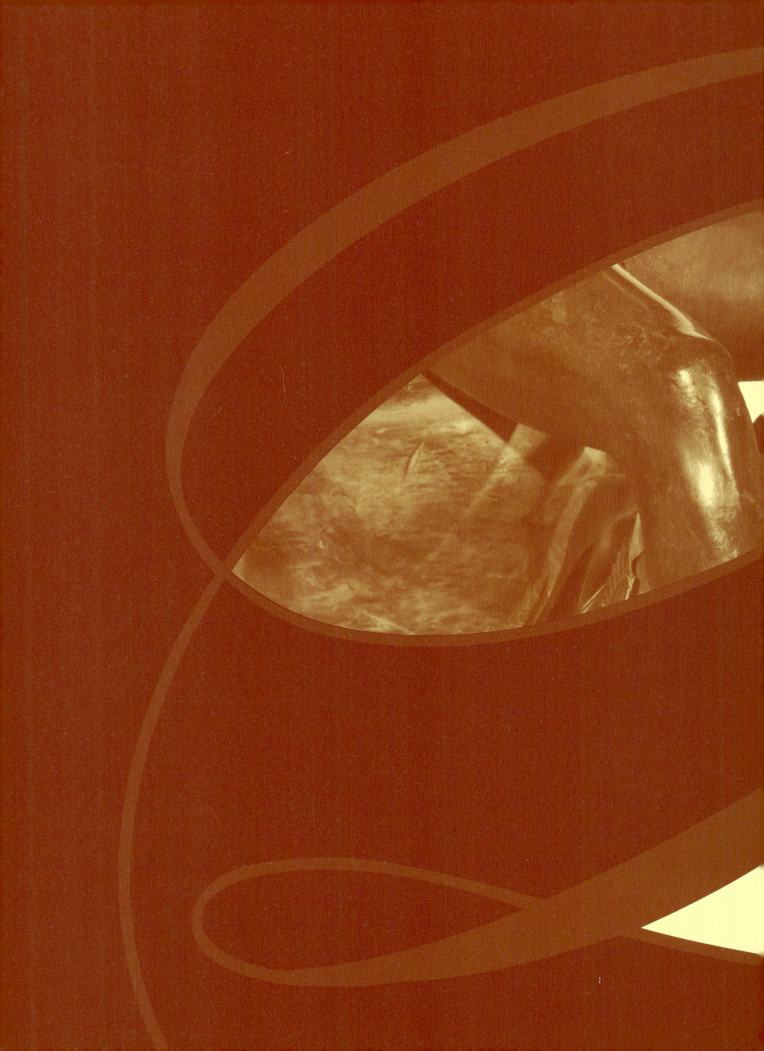

梦回盛世

Dreaming of a Great Era

庞贝，公元前 6 世纪初建城，公元前 89 年被古罗马人征服。在古希腊和古罗马文明的影响下，庞贝逐渐发展成具有一定规模的城市。虽然不能与罗马和雅典这样的大城市相比，但庞贝和赫库兰尼姆已经是两座相当发达的城市，经济发展迅速，城市建设高度发展，人民生活富足，艺术创造也达到了极高的水平。

然而，公元 79 年，维苏威火山喷发后短短几个小时内，它们就都被掩埋了。但也因为被掩埋在厚厚的火山灰下，那里的房屋、物品、壁画和艺术品都保存得极为完好，作为古罗马人生活的绝佳象征，静静地在时空中凝结。

Pompeii, founded in the early 6th century BC, was conquered by the ancient Romans in 89 BC and gradually developed, under both Greek and Roman civilizations, into a city of a certain scale. Although not comparable to larger cities such as Rome and Athens, Pompeii and Herculaneum were already two well-developed cities with rapid economic growth, high urban expansion, an affluent population and an advanced level of artistic creation.

However, in the short space of a few hours, they were buried by the eruption of Mount Vesuvius in 79 AD Due to being buried under a thick layer of ash, the houses, objects, frescoes and works of art were preserved in excellent condition, quietly suspended in time and becoming the best representation of Roman life of that time.

带我去庞贝吧，那里有甜蜜的爱情。

POMPEIOS DEFER, VBI DVLCIS EST AMOR

Take me to Pompeii, where love is sweet

庞贝古城与赫库兰尼姆古城
Pompeii and Herculaneum

本展览首先呈现的是两座古城的标志性建筑——纸莎草别墅和农牧神之家。它们是庞贝与赫库兰尼姆神话之美的主要表现。纸莎草别墅位于赫库兰尼姆，因在其中发现的1826张纸莎草纸而得名。别墅矗立在海边，绘有许多以小爱神和海洋动物为主题的壁画，并饰以多尊大理石和青铜雕像。其中，于本展览展出的《赫耳墨斯坐像》，完美代表着这座古罗马别墅中的丰富艺术藏品。

庞贝古城中的私人建筑农牧神之家，则达到了极高的华丽精致程度。这座建筑中珍贵的壁画装饰、马赛克和雕像琳琅满目。入口处地板上的马赛克图案用拉丁语"HAVE"（你好）表达着对来客的欢迎、接纳和关注。

The exhibition begins from two emblematic buildings of the ancient cities, the main containers of beauty in the myth of Pompeii and Herculaneum: the Villa of the Papyri and the House of the Faun. The Villa of the Papyri is so named because of the one thousand eight hundred and twenty-six papyri found inside it. Located in Herculaneum, it stood overlooking the sea and was richly decorated with frescoes of cupids and sea animals as well as marble and bronze statues such as the *Seated Hermes* on display here.

With the House of the Faun in Pompeii, private construction reached a high level of opulence and refinement, with precious frescoed decorations, mosaics, and statues. The entrance to this house bears a floor mosaic with a word in Latin which welcomes the guest as a sign of openness and interest: HAVE.

庞贝古城
Pompeii

赫库兰尼姆古城
Herculaneum

众神使者：赫耳墨斯
Messenger of the Gods: Hermes

奥林匹斯之神赫耳墨斯是宙斯和迈亚之子，担任着众神使者的角色。赫耳墨斯的鞋有双翼，能够以极快的速度旅行，因此他成为商业之神与旅行的保护神。除此以外，赫耳墨斯还是亡灵的接引神，护送逝者的灵魂到达冥界。

因为赫耳墨斯拥有的众多特征，如精明、口才以及身体和思想上的敏捷，荷马将他形容为"polýtropos"，即"拥有多种资源"，由此巩固了他的多面形象。在古典时代，赫耳墨斯被描绘成一个没有胡须的裸体青年，手持蛇缠绕的手杖，穿着神奇的有翼鞋，戴着独特的有翼宽边帽。

那不勒斯国家考古博物馆的这件赫耳墨斯坐像有着独一无二的呈现视角。它依据古罗马时期的复制品而制，原件可能源自公元前2世纪的古希腊时期。作品中只穿着翼鞋的人物保持着坐姿，凝神专注，这似乎与本尊的好动天性相矛盾。这尊雕塑是在纸莎草别墅的柱廊中被发现的。在当时，它很可能为别墅的客人们营造着快乐和休闲的氛围。

An Olympian deity, son of Zeus and the nymph Maia, Hermes held the role of messenger of the gods. Equipped with winged footwear that enabled him to travel extremely fast, he became a protective figure of trade and travel, including that to the realm of the dead, where he accompanied the souls of the departed.

His traits, such as shrewdness, eloquence, and quickness both physically and in thought, cause Homer to define him as *polýtropos*, of many resources, consolidating his image as a multifaceted character. In the classical age Hermes is depicted as a naked, beardless youth who can hold a caduceus, a staff wrapped in snakes, and wear both the mythical winged footwear and the petasus, a distinctive headdress.

Singular from the point of view of representation is this sculpture from the Museo Archeologico Nazionale di Napoli, created according to a Roman copy of a Greek original, probably from the 2nd century BC which seems to contradict its dynamic nature by representing him seated and absorbed, dressed only in his shoes. Found in the peristyle of the Villa of the Papyri it probably reinforced that idea of *otium* (pleasure, leisure) that the place must have continually suggested to its guests.

赫耳墨斯坐像（复制品）

青铜
2022 年
125cm×112cm×78cm

本展品为赫库兰尼姆纸莎草别墅中发现的
青铜雕像的现代复制品。可追溯至公元前 1
世纪的原雕像，很有可能是古罗马人对公
元前 2 世纪希腊雕像的复制品。作品中，赫
耳墨斯被描绘成坐在岩石上的少年。他右
腿伸直，左腿向后弯曲，身体微微前倾，左
臂撑在左大腿上，右臂搭在身旁的岩石上。
他左手中的短杆可能是有翼双蛇杖的一部
分。赫耳墨斯赤着身体，鞋上有双翼。有
翼鞋能够助他以极快的速度旅行，履行他
作为众神使者的职责。此刻，赫耳墨斯正
稍作休息，陷入沉思，目光向下凝视。

Seated Hermes (replica)

Bronze
2022
125cm×112cm×78cm

A modern replica of the bronze statue found in the Villa of the Papyri in Herculaneum. The
original statue dates to the 1st century BC and is possibly a Roman copy of a Greek original from
the 2nd century BC. Hermes is depicted as a young adolescent sitting on a rock with his right leg
extended and his left leg bent backwards. He leans slightly forwards, with his left arm leaning on
his left thigh and his right arm resting on the rock beside him. In his left hand he holds a short
rod, possibly what remains of a caduceus, a winged staff with two coiled snakes. Hermes is naked
but for the winged sandals on his feet, known as talaria, which allowed him to travel extremely
fast and fulfil his role as messenger of the gods. He is caught in a moment of rest and reflection,
depicted with his face absorbed as suggested by his downward gaze.

纸莎草别墅
The Villa of the Papyri

纸莎草别墅是一座古罗马建筑，很可能属盖乌斯·尤利乌斯·恺撒的岳父所有。别墅建于公元前 60 至前 50 年之间。稍早于 1750 年时，它在赫库兰尼姆被发现。多年以来，人们对这处遗址进行了多次挖掘，且挖掘工作尚未完全完成，这一点也证明了这座建筑的宏大规模。

纸莎草别墅共有四层，由四个主体部分构成，其中包括一个带图书馆的住宅区。正是这座图书馆中的 1826 卷纸莎草纸卷——主要用希腊语写成的哲学书籍，赋予别墅这个家喻户晓的名字。如此大量的著作使我们明白，学习、知识和文化在当时被认为是真正的乐趣。

如果说别墅客人的心灵被纸莎草纸上的文字所滋养，那么他们的视觉则参与着一场无数具象艺术作品构成的盛宴。别墅绘有精美的建筑壁画，而有史以来在私人住宅中发现的最丰富的雕塑群则沿着中庭和柱廊排列，其中有 58 尊青铜雕像和 21 尊大理石雕像。

别墅中发掘出的家具和陈设，也由于其珍贵性和精美的做工，揭示着此地的本质：这是个不管从感官的愉悦还是从理智的乐趣上，都意在充分体现奢华的空间。

The Villa of the Papyri is a Roman building probably belonging to the father-in-law of Gaius Julius Caesar, built between 60 and 50 BC and discovered in Herculaneum shortly before 1750. Over the years there were several excavation campaigns, not yet fully completed, which confirm the grandeur of the building.

Arranged on four levels, it consists of four sections including living quarters with a library. The very contents of the latter, 1826 papyrus scrolls, mostly written in Greek and dealing with philosophy, contributed to the name by which the villa became known. The presence of such a large number of writings makes us understand that study, knowledge and culture were considered as real "pleasures".

If the minds of the villa's guests were nourished by the writings of the papyri, their eyes were satisfied by the presence of numerous works of figurative art. Fantastic architecture stood out on the walls, while along atriums and peristyles was arranged the richest series of sculptures ever found in a private home: 58 bronze and 21 marble statues.

Even the furniture and furnishings found, due to their extraordinary preciousness and workmanship, reveal the nature of this place: a space created to fully embody luxury, based on sensory but also cerebral pleasure.

5619 号女舞者（复制品）

青铜
2022 年
157cm × 80cm × 41cm

赫库兰尼姆的纸莎草别墅中曾发现一组五位女子的群雕、这尊现代青铜雕像复制品是这组群雕中的一部分。群雕中的五位年轻女性呈站姿，身着多立克式披肩、肩带扣在肩上。她们面部精致但稍显僵硬、眼神灵活。眼睛中角膜的部分由骨头或象牙制成，虹膜和瞳孔由灰色或黑色石头制成。18 世纪时，这组雕像曾被德国考古学家温克尔曼错误地命名为"女舞者们"，随后又在 19 世纪被命名为"运水者"，最后在 20 世纪被确认为利比亚国王达那俄斯的女儿——国王的五十个女儿在杀死各自的丈夫后，被罚永不停歇地运水。作品的结构几乎是建筑式的，长袍质感坚硬，上面有类似于希腊柱身的深槽。不过，这种形式上的僵硬感被女子们各自不同的优雅手势和姿态所冲淡了，群雕的各尊雕像中，身体的重量、手臂的姿势和发型都各不相同。

Dancer 5619 (replica)

Bronze
2022
157cm × 80cm × 41cm

A modern replica of a bronze statue, part of a group of five found in the Villa of the Papyri in Herculaneum. The group represents five young standing women dressed in Doric peplos buckled on the shoulders and portrayed in different postures and hairstyles. The faces are delicate but rigid and have animated eyes, the corneas of which are made of bone or ivory and the iris and pupils of grey or black stone. They are defined mistakenly as dancers by Winckelmann in the 18th century, followed by hydrophorai (water carriers) in the 19th century and finally identified in the 20th century as the Danaids, the fifty daughters of Danaus the king of Libya, condemned to fetch water for eternity after killing their respective husbands. The structure of the sculptures appears almost architectural, with the solid robes having deep grooves similar to those of the column shafts. The rigidity of the forms is, however, diluted by the variety and elegance of the women's gestures and poses, which differ in the weighting of the body, in the arrangement of the arms and in the articulation of the hair.

醉酒之神西勒努斯灯座（复制品）

青铜
20 世纪初
61cm × 30cm

西勒努斯是森林中的小神，性情狂野好色，是
酒神文化中的典型人物。本展品中，西勒努斯
的形象被使用在灯座上。对于古人来说，油灯
发出的光是宴会的特色之一，因为在当时，油
灯是使用最多的照明方式，而酒神狄俄尼索斯
则是宴会的守护神。

Silenus lamp holder (replica)

Bronze
Early 20th century
61cm × 30cm

Silenus is a minor deity of the woods, of a
wild and lascivious nature, a typical figure of
the world of Dionysus. He is depicted here as
a support for an oil lamp. For the ancients, the
light coming from the oil lamps characterised
their banquets, because it was the most
commonly used lighting system. The figure
of Silenus ties back with Dionysus being the
tutelary deity of banquets.

带翼的胜利女神（复制品）

青铜
20 世纪初
65cm × 47cm × 47cm

本展品为庞贝古城出土的一尊精致小雕像的现代复制品，呈现的是胜利女神。行进中的她，左脚踩在下方的圆球上，右脚在后。女神展开大的翅膀，身穿古希腊式长衣。面料巧妙地呈现着动态，紧贴着支撑的左腿，产生了许多古代女性雕像所特有的"湿面料"效果。女神蓬松的头发上戴着王冠，伸出的右臂和弯曲的左臂很可能各自持着一顶王冠和一面旗帜。

Winged Victory (replica)

Bronze
Early 20th century
65cm × 47cm × 47cm

A modern replica of a small but refined figurine found in Pompeii and depicting the female goddess Victory, advancing with the left foot on a small globe and the right foot set back. The goddess has large open wings and wears a peplos, the fabric of which is masterfully rendered as moving, adhering to the supporting leg and causing the effect of the so-called 'wet' fabric characteristic of many ancient female figures. The hairstyle is swollen with a diadem in the hair. The outstretched right arm and the left bent presumably supported a crown and a banner.

农牧神之家
The House of the Faun

农牧神之家这座豪华住宅占地约 3000 平方米，是庞贝最大的住宅之一。人们来到用拉丁文铭文欢迎客人的住宅入口处，已经可以感受到主人颇高的社会地位。

这座住宅内部甚至配有温泉洗浴系统，房子的每个空间都展示着富有和华丽。在众多装饰品中，尤为突出的是以尼罗河为主要场景的壁画，它们明显是受到埃及风格的影响。同样精美的还有描绘伊苏斯战役的地板马赛克画，制作它时使用了近一百五十万块瓷砖。

在农牧神之家的众多艺术品中，最具代表性的仍然是放置在主中庭承雨池中央的小青铜雕像。雕像呈现的是正在起舞的森林之神萨提尔（satyr），或称农牧神。"农牧神之家"的名字正来源于此，它也暗暗寓含着主人的家族名称——萨特里（Satrii）。

Sumptuous *domus*, among the largest in Pompeii, it occupies an entire block of about 3,000 square meters. From the very entrance to the house, preceded by the Latin inscription of welcome, HAVE, one perceives the high social standing of the owner.

Every space in the residence, which even has a domestic bath system, reveals opulence and splendour, especially in the numerous decorations among which stand out the walls painted with scenes of subjects known as "Nilotic", figures revealing an Egyptian influence, and the extraordinary floor mosaic in the tablinum depicting the Battle of Issus; it appears that nearly a million and a half pieces were used to create it.

But the most representative work of art in the domus remains the small bronze statue placed in the centre of the impluvium of the main atrium that depicts a dancing satyr, or faun, from which derives the name of the house and which alludes to the lineage of the owners: the Satrii.

起舞的农牧神
The Dancing Faun

农牧神之家因这座在其内部发现的小型青铜雕塑而命名。雕塑位于承雨池中央，为留有胡须的裸体男性形象。他的头向后仰，目光朝上，似乎要踮起脚尖翩翩起舞。

这个形象有一系列的明显特征，例如山羊角和尾巴，这使它看上去像农牧神（与农林业有关的仁慈生物）或希腊神话中的萨提尔。萨提尔的形象比农牧神更放纵，主要表现着本能和欲望。

在庞贝的这座雕像中，这些生物的兽性特征其实已被削弱了。它们更常见的形象实则在形态和姿势上都显出更多的动物性——通常是不守规矩、充满欲望的。基督教中的魔鬼形象有很大可能就来源于这些形象。

This small bronze sculpture gives its name to the domus within which it was found. Placed in the centre of the *impluvium*, it depicts a bearded, nude male figure who, with his head tipped back and looking upward, seems to be hinting at a dance step on the tip of his toes.

The figure is distinguished by a series of attributes, such as horns and a goat's tail, that identify it with a faun, a benevolent creature connected to the agricultural and woodland world, or even a satyr, a deity of the Greek world who represents a more unrestrained declination of the faun, linked more to instincts and lust.

While the Pompeian statue attenuates the animalistic attributes that characterize these beings, the more usual manner by which these creatures are represented shows more of their animalistic nature both in their forms and in their poses, which are often dishevelled, almost lascivious. The Christian iconography of the devil probably originates precisely from this type of representation.

起舞的农牧神（复制品）

青铜
2022 年
83cm × 25cm × 30cm

这尊现代制作的雕像是公元前 2 世纪原作的复制品，它装饰着庞贝古城农牧神之家位于中庭中央的承雨池。雕像呈现的是一位留着胡须的裸体男性。他的头向后倾斜，欣喜的目光朝向上方，尾巴和头发呈现飘逸状态。人物头上的角和小的尾巴表明这个人物的身份是农牧神、潘神，或者更确切地说，是正在跳舞的萨提尔。人物踮起脚尖，似乎要翩翩起舞。这尊小型青铜器的制作极为精良，以坚实的肌肉组织展现高超的技巧和柔软度，身体的结构又与人物整体的螺旋动态完美对应。

The dancing faun (replica)

Bronze
2022
83cm × 25cm × 30cm

This modern example is a replica of the 2nd century BC original which decorated the impluvium at the centre of the atrium of the House of the Faun in Pompeii. The statue depicted a naked male and bearded figure, his head tilted back, his ecstatic gaze facing upwards, his tail and locks flowing. The presence of horns on the head and the small tail identify the figure as a faun, the god Pan, or rather a dancing satyr depicted hinting, on tiptoe, a dance step. The small bronze presents a particular refinement of technical execution, with the solid musculature rendered with great skill and softness and the anatomy of the body perfectly corresponding to the spiral movement involving the figure as a whole.

古希腊罗马时期的爱情神话

Love in Greco-Roman Mythology

爱情，是古典时代永恒的主题。古希腊、古罗马先人把因爱而生的渴望、痴迷、痛苦与迷惘都注入了神话之中。一个个有血有肉的神话人物形象，呈现出爱情这一宏大主题丰富的层次和深刻的内涵。爱，以多种不同的呈现形态，在古希腊、古罗马文化体系中占据着中心地位。

阿佛洛狄忒是希腊神话中代表爱和美的女神，在罗马时期被称作维纳斯。她拥有古希腊最完美的身段和容颜，是爱情的化身。在本单元中，观众可以一览爱情女神从海中诞生时的灿烂之姿。她肌肤胜雪、面容恬静，以优雅的姿态沐浴出水，这一经典的画面影响了整个古代和现代的西方艺术。

阿佛洛狄忒的其中四个儿子被称为厄洛特斯，代表着四种不同的爱。这四个儿子分别是爱神厄洛斯、代表情欲的希莫勒斯、代表相爱的安忒洛斯，以及象征思恋之爱的波索斯。本单元展出的波索斯雕像极为珍贵，它象征着因爱而不得所生出的渴望，更确切地说，是因为爱情触不可及而带来的遗憾、留恋与期盼，是"会令人软弱的对爱的无比渴望"。

Love, the eternal theme of classical times. The ancestors of ancient Greece and Rome infused mythology with the longing, obsession, pain and confusion that is born from love. The flesh and blood of each mythical figure reveals the rich layers and profound connotations of the grand theme of love. Thus love, in its many different forms of representation, occupies a central place in the ancient Greek and Roman systems of culture and thought.

Aphrodite is the goddess of love and beauty in Greek mythology, known as Venus in Roman times. With the most perfect figure and face of ancient Greece, she is the embodiment of love. In this exhibition section, viewers can see the goddess in all her splendour as she is born from the sea. With her snowy skin and serene face, she emerges from the water in a graceful pose, a classic image that has influenced Western art throughout antiquity and modern times.

Four sons of Aphrodite are collectively known as Erotes, representing four different kinds of love. These four sons are Eros, the god of love, Himeros, who represents amorous lust, Anteros, the god of requited love, and Pothos, who symbolises the nostalgia and longing for love. The statue of Pothos, which is on display here, is a precious symbol of the longing that comes from not being able to love, or more precisely, the regret, longing and expectation that comes from love being out of reach, the 'overwhelming longing for love that can be debilitating'.

愿有爱之人，福寿绵长；

无爱之人，死不足惜；

禁爱之人，罪不容诛。

QVIS AMAT VALEAT PEREAT QVI

NESCIT AMARE BIS TANTI PEREAT

QVISQVIS AMARE VETAT

Whoever loves, may they flourish
Whoever knows not how to love may they perish
Whoever forbids love, may they perish twice

爱神厄洛斯
Eros: God of Love

在古希腊和古罗马时期，追求爱情并不是一种需要被抑制的罪恶，而是人的生命活力和尊严的体现。古希腊、古罗马的神祇，也和当时的人们一样，充盈着对生命原欲的追求。其中最为人所熟知的爱神即为丘比特，而在希腊神话中，他被称为厄洛斯。因此，在当时的文化和思想体系中，爱情占据着中心地位，其不同形式体现在文化和思想的方方面面。

厄洛斯或丘比特的形象是带有武器的少年神，其弓弦上经常射出致命的箭矢，受其影响的人则将无路可逃，坠入爱河。他不仅是情感的人格化体现，更代表强烈的欲望。情感和欲望是爱情的两面，但在古典时代，它们则作为人类体验的两个独立时刻而被看待。

爱神是不遵循规则的。这并不是说这些规则对凡人不存在。相反，它们存在着，并且极为严格。例如，未婚女性必须严格遵守贞操；已婚女性必须同样严格地保有忠诚。但爱神并不重视规则，而是同样地在凡人、神灵、半人、动物、男人和女人之间创造出爱。

In the ancient Greek and Roman world, the pursuit of love was not a sin to be suppressed, but an expression of the vitality and dignity of human life. The gods of ancient Greece and Rome, like the people of that time, were also filled with the pursuit of the original desire for life. One of the most well-known gods of love was Cupid, called Eros by the Greeks. Thus, love occupied a central position in the cultural and intellectual system of the time, and its many forms were reflected in all aspects of culture and thought.

Cupid was represented as an armed child-god who shot arrows with his bow. Those struck by it had no chance: they fell in love. But Cupid did not only personify the feeling of love, but also passionate desire. These were the two faces of love, feeling and desire, which, however, were experienced in classical antiquity as two separate moments of human experience.

Eros knew no rules but for mortals they existed and were very strict: for example, unmarried women were required to have strict chastity, and married women were required to have strict fidelity. But Eros did not care about rules and made love arise, indifferently, between mortal beings, gods, semi-human figures, animals, men and women.

有爱神与酒神图案的钟形红绘双柄大口罐

陶
公元前 5 世纪末
34cm × 36cm

这种有特殊造型的典型希腊式罐子叫做钟形大口罐。
也就是说，它的形状像一口倒置的钟，边缘呈喇叭
形，杯脚较矮，黑色背景上装饰有红色和白色图案。
图案描绘的是狂喜和陶醉之神狄俄尼索斯，以及爱神
阿佛洛狄忒的儿子、代表肉体之爱的厄洛斯。

Bell krater with Eros and Dionysus

Pottery
Late 5th century BC
34cm × 36cm

A classic example of a Greek vessel with a particular
shape called a bell krater. It is in the shape of an inverted
bell and has a flared rim, raised on a foot with a short
stem and two handles pointing upwards. Decorated with
a technique called red-figure, it has mostly red figures and
some white figures on a black background. The scenes
depict Dionysus, god of ecstasy and intoxication, and Eros,
son of Aphrodite, god of physical love.

有爱神图案的陶酒瓶

陶
公元前 4 世纪
26cm × 16cm

这种希腊式陶酒瓶有着古老的起源，有各种各样的形状和装饰。这里展现的是最富变化的形式，黑色背景上的红色人物是代表肉体之爱的厄洛斯。

Oinochoe with Eros

Pottery
4th century BC
26cm × 16cm

The oinochoe is a jug-like vessel used to hold wine. Of very ancient origin, it has taken on a great variety of shapes and decorations. This example is in its most evolved form with red figures on a black background and depicts Eros, god of physical love.

有爱神图案的内斯特瓶

陶
公元前 4 世纪
44cm × 37cm

这种造型独特容器的手柄节点处有小圆盘。意大利南部的陶器绝大部分是雅典式的，但内斯特瓶却是一种本土的器型，主要在阿普利亚和卢卡尼亚两个地区制作。作为宴会用的容器，它很能显示身份地位，用于非常正式的欢庆时刻，对当地重要人物和权威人士来说非常重要。这件展品饰有爱神的图案，黑色背景上绘有红色的人物形象。

Nestoris with Eros

Pottery
4ᵗʰ century BC
44cm × 37cm

The nestoris is a vase with an unmistakable shape due to the presence of small discs in the nodes of the handles. While most shapes in South Italian vase-painting depend on Attic models, the nestoris is indigenous, produced mainly in Apulia and Lucania. It had a strong identity value as a banquet form used for very formal moments of conviviality and of great importance to the community for the ruling elites. This specimen is decorated with stories of Eros with red figures on a black background.

有爱神图案的双耳细颈罐

陶
公元前 4 世纪
35cm × 22cm

这种宽口罐用于盛放液体。它最宽的部分是底部，有两个竖着的带状手柄。罐体黑色背景上的红色人物是雌雄同体的爱神。

Pelike with Eros

Pottery
4th century BC
35cm × 22cm

The pelike is type of vessel with a wide mouth. Used to hold liquids, it has a sagging belly and vertical ribbon-like handles on either side. The red figures on a black background here depict Eros represented as a hermaphrodite.

阿佛洛狄忒：爱与美的化身
Aphrodite: Embodiment of Love and Beauty

在古希腊文化中，爱情体验是受到阿佛洛狄忒保护的。阿佛洛狄忒女神主掌快乐与两性的结合，是位出色的诱惑者。这位强大的女神诞生于大海的白色泡沫中，她美丽而闪亮的诗意形象，在古代艺术及现代艺术中都极富魅力。

在塞浦路斯地区，人们普遍崇拜阿佛洛狄忒，这能证实她的形象是源自东方的。中东地区普遍崇拜的巴比伦女神伊什塔尔的形象，几乎是阿佛洛狄忒的原版。她们都代表着金星，也同样主管着与情爱和生育相关的力量。

无论是在婚姻领域还是在自由关系中，女性都会因为爱情和性的问题向阿佛洛狄忒求助。通常来说，少女们会向阿佛洛狄忒祈祷赐予她们丈夫，或感谢她让自己得偿所愿，并供奉给她衣物、珠宝和装饰品。

阿佛洛狄忒是伟大爱情的主角，她是跛脚的火神与锻造之神赫菲斯托斯的妻子，她的情人是迷人而又凶猛残酷的战神阿瑞斯。阿佛洛狄忒与美少年阿多尼斯这位无法抗拒的诱惑者也有过火热的爱情。他们的关系激起了阿瑞斯的愤怒，在一次狩猎旅行中，阿瑞斯放出一头野猪来攻击阿多尼斯，使他伤重而亡。

阿佛洛狄忒与战神阿瑞斯爱抚和拥抱的形象周围，经常有厄洛斯们环绕。厄洛斯们将神的可怕武器变成天真的游戏，不再只呈现爱情本身享有特权和挑衅的形象，而更强调阿佛洛狄忒的强大力量——她用温柔但非常坚韧的美和爱的关系约束着战争和死亡。

阿佛洛狄忒情人众多，因而生育了很多孩子，包括特洛伊的英雄埃涅阿斯。而儿子爱神厄洛斯则是与她最著名的情人——战神阿瑞斯生育的。不幸嫁与火神赫菲斯托斯而寄托于婚外情的这种倾向，使阿佛洛狄忒在古希腊成为感官陶醉的象征，被视作一种能够压倒和约束宇宙的力量。但随着柏拉图著作的出现，这种观点也发生了变化。柏拉图在《会饮篇》中将阿佛洛狄忒分为两种神格的女神：天上的纯爱女神代表着精神上的纯洁理想之爱；地上的情爱女神及娼妓的保护神则代表着自由和肉体之爱。

这种对同一神祇怀有的矛盾心理也反映在阿佛洛狄忒的肖像画中。古希腊雕刻家菲迪亚斯的"纯爱女神阿佛洛狄忒"因流传至今的复制品而为人所知。如果说，这尊雕像还被庄严地包裹在古希腊式长袍中，那么从古希腊雕刻家普拉克西特列斯开始，则更加流行女神的裸体形象雕塑，以彰显其美丽和性感。这些裸体形象可能明显带有情色特征，如在雕像"露出美臀的阿佛洛狄忒"中，女神掀起紧身衣，露出自己的臀部和腰身。或者，像那不勒斯国家考古博物馆藏有的这尊雕像那样，根据希腊化时代流行的姿势，低调但性感地在不经意间展示着胸部和耻骨。

The experience of love in Greek and Roman culture is placed under the auspices of Aphrodite, the goddess who is responsible for the sphere of pleasure and sexual union: she is the seductress par excellence. Aphrodite is a most powerful goddess, born of the white foam of the sea, beautiful and resplendent, a poetic image that will fascinate ancient and modern artistic tradition.

The widespread diffusion of the cult in the Cypriot area confirms the eastern origin of her figure, overlapping with that of the Babylonian Ishtar especially with regard to the exercise of intercourse as a power related to fertility.

Women turn to Aphrodite for what pertains to the love and sexual sphere, whether in the marital sphere or in free relationships: these are often maidens who pray to Aphrodite to grant them a husband or to thank her for obtaining one by giving her clothing, jewellery and ornaments.

Aphrodite is the protagonist of great loves: wife of Hephaestus, the cripple god of fire and metallurgy, she had as her lover the handsome Ares, fierce and cruel god of war. A passionate love was also that for Adonis, handsome and irresistible seducer: their relationship aroused the wrath of Ares, who during a hunting party unleashed a boar at the young man, mortally wounding him.

The caresses and embraces between Aphrodite and Ares, god of war, often surrounded by heroes who transform the god's fearsome weapons into innocent playthings, far from representing exclusively the privileged and provocative image of the physicality of love, emphasize above all the power and strength of the goddess, who enchains with sweet but very strong laces of beauty and love the instruments of war and death.

From her numerous romantic liaisons she had, in fact, many children, including the Trojan hero Aeneas as well as Eros, god of love, conceived with Ares. This aptitude for extramarital affairs on the part of the goddess, unhappily married to Hephaestus, made her, in the archaic Greek world, a symbolic figure of the thrill of the senses understood as a power capable of investing and binding all parts of the Universe. This view changed with Plato who, in his Ethics, distinguished her into two parts: Aphrodite Urania, a celestial and spiritual figure, the expression of pure and ideal love, and Aphrodite Pandemia, who evoked free and carnal love so much so that prostitutes invoked her as their protector.

This ambivalence will also be reflected in the iconography adopted to represent the goddess. If, in fact, Phidias' Aphrodite Urania, known through the copies that have come down to us, was solemnly wrapped in a himation (a mantle or wrap), from Praxiteles onward images spread that saw the deity naked in order to enhance her beauty and voluptuousness. Such figures could be distinctly erotic, such as the Aphrodite Callipyge which uncovers her buttocks and hips by lifting her *peplos* (body-length garment), or, according to a pose that spread in the Hellenistic age, modest, though always sensual, depicted while negligently covering her breasts and pubis as is the case in the sculpture of the Museo Archeologico Nazionale di Napoli collection.

海中的阿佛洛狄忒

大理石
公元 1 世纪
120cm×51cm×30cm

这件作品中，阿佛洛狄忒呈站姿，身体的重量放在左腿上，右膝盖弯曲。她直视前方，左臂支撑在臀部，右手倚放在杆上。女神身穿古希腊式的短袍，衣服紧贴在身上，表明她刚刚浮出水面。一件较厚的长袍遮住了她的下半身。根据神话，阿佛洛狄忒诞生于大海的泡沫中，她打湿的衣袍也显示着这一点。

Aphrodite Marina

Marble
1st century AD
120cm×51cm×30cm

Aphrodite is here depicted standing, her left leg bearing her weight and her right leg bent at the knee. She looks straight ahead, her left arm resting on her hip, her right arm leaning on a pole. The goddess is wearing a thin tunic which hugs her forms, suggesting she has just emerged from the water. A thicker robe hides her lower half. According to myth, Aphrodite was born from the foam of the sea, an aspect of her legend that is suggested by her wet tunic.

公元 2 世纪
180cm × 70cm × 67cm

阿佛洛狄忒在古罗马时期的形象是多种多样的，这座雕塑呈现的是其中一种。爱神阿佛洛狄忒也是生命力和生育力的象征。本展品中，爱神以全裸的形象出现，以左腿为支撑站立着，双手遮住耻骨和左侧胸部。画面右边，一块简单的布搭在花瓶上。女神的头部向左转，发型精致。高处的头发在头顶打结，其余的头发聚集在颈背，还有几绺头发垂在肩上。

Aphrodite Capitolina

Marble
2nd century AD
180cm × 70cm × 67cm

The sculpture represents Aphrodite, goddess of love and symbol of life force and fertility, in one of many Roman variants. The goddess of love, completely nude, stands on her left leg and is caught in the act of covering her pubis and left breast; on the right a simple drape resting on a vase serves as a support. The head, turned towards the left, is characterised by an elaborate hairstyle, with higher locks knotted vexatiously at the top of the head and the remaining ones gathered at the nape of the neck from which some locks fall to the shoulders.

波索斯：触不可及的爱情
Pothos: Untouchable Love

波索斯是阿佛洛狄忒和柯罗诺斯的儿子，厄洛斯的兄弟。他代表着对心爱之人的爱意，也代表着无法实现的或理想化的爱情。

大约在公元前 5 世纪，波索斯的特征在文学和哲学中渐渐确立。柏拉图尤其将他视作对无法征服的事物的渴望。波索斯被描绘成带翅膀的赤裸少年，常以站立并倚靠某物的形象出现，以凸显其忧郁本性。这种形象在古希腊时期固定了下来。

在几乎所有的雕塑复制品中，波索斯都有相同的姿态，包括来自意大利那不勒斯国家考古博物馆的这座雕塑。作品曲折的构图使人联想到美惠三女神，即美丽与优雅的混合体，而这正是波索斯的特征。因为并不代表奥林匹斯之神的神性，波索斯可以摆脱神们典型的严谨特质，呈现更人性的一面，少了理想化的特征，而多了浪漫的美。

Son of Aphrodite and Chronos, Pothos represents amorous desire, a form of longing for the beloved. A component of the Erotes, personifications of feelings related to love of which Eros, his brother, is the main exponent, he also embodies unattainable or idealized love.

His characteristics become established in literature and philosophy in about the 5th century BC, particularly in Plato, who assimilates him to the yearning desire for what cannot be conquered, while his iconography, which sees him as a winged and naked adolescent, frequently depicted standing but leaning toward a support to emphasize his melancholic nature, is consolidated in the Hellenistic age.

The same pose is found in almost all sculptural replicas of the subject, including this one from the Museo Archeologico Nazionale di Napoli, without going astray. Precisely because of the sinuosity of the composition, there remains a reference to that chàris, a mixture of beauty and grace, which characterizes Pothos who, not representing an Olympian divinity, can shed the rigor typical of these subjects to associate himself with a more "human", less idealized but more romantic beauty.

波索斯

大理石
公元 2 世纪
218cm × 75cm × 51cm

本展品呈现的形象是波索斯，是对远方爱人思念的化身。他呈站立姿态，以右腿为支撑，弯曲的左腿则交叉在右腿上，仅脚趾着地。波索斯的身体倾向左方，这种不平衡的姿势使得负重一侧的髋部更加弯曲，左肩也因而抬高。为了延长骨盆和肩部连成的斜线，他的右臂向前放在胸前，同时左臂高举。斗篷从左臂上笔直地垂下来，落在一只鹅的背上。

Pothos

Marble
2nd century AD
218cm × 75cm × 51cm

The figure is that of Pothos, the personification of yearning for the distant loved one. He is depicted standing, gravitating on the right leg, while the flexed left leg crosses the other, resting only with the toe on the ground. The torso is unbalanced to the left, in an attitude that accentuates the flexion of the hip on the weight-bearing side, with the counterpoint of the raised left shoulder. To prolong the oblique lines of the pelvis and shoulders, the right arm is brought forward on the chest, while the left is raised high; from this the cloak falls rigidly plumb, on the back of a goose.

人神之爱：神话中的爱情故事
The Love Between Man and God: Love Stories in Mythology

古希腊和古罗马神话中的爱情不尽相同，往往涉及神祇和凡人，为着神和人之间本不该存在的爱情创造可能。

月亮女神塞勒涅每天驾驶着她的战车穿越苍穹。某次，她偶然遇见恩底弥翁，爱上了这位正在小憩的俊美牧羊人。一个是不朽之神，一个身为凡人，他们的爱情不可能长存，因此，塞勒涅请求天神宙斯保留恩底弥翁的容貌。恩底弥翁由此长睡不醒，永葆青春俊美，每晚都被他的爱人塞勒涅所仰慕。

众神与凡人间的爱情，往往因后者的美貌而起，宙斯与伽倪墨得斯、宙斯与勒达之间都是如此。宙斯为这两个凡人的美貌着迷，化身为一只老鹰，将美少年伽倪墨得斯带到奥林匹斯山，让他成为自己的挚爱；又化身为一只天鹅，去引诱斯巴达的王后勒达。宙斯和勒达的爱情结晶则是著名的美人——引发了特洛伊战争的海伦。

Love in Greek and Roman mythology finds different forms, often including both gods and mortals, finding solutions for a love that should not exist: a love between mortals and immortals.

Selene, personification of the moon, has the task of crossing the sky every day with her chariot. During one of these crossings she falls in love with Endymion, a beautiful shepherd resting. She, immortal with a task to perform, he, mortal, created a love that could not exist. So Selene pleads with Zeus to preserve him as he was. Endymion would never wake up again, remaining eternally young and beautiful, admired every night by his love Selene.

Love between gods and mortals is often due to the latter's beauty, as is also the case between Zeus and Ganymede and Zeus and Leda. Zeus, enamoured by the beauty of the two mortals, transformed himself into an eagle to bring the boy Ganymede to Olympus and make him his beloved, and into a swan to seduce Leda, queen of Sparta, from which union Helen was born.

没有你，
哪怕我成了神，
也终将湮灭。

PEREAM SINE TE SI DEVS ESSE VELIM

Let me perish without you if I should wish
to be a god

塞勒涅与恩底弥翁

壁画
公元 1 世纪
71cm×71cm×8cm

在赫库兰尼姆古城出土的这幅壁画中，恩底弥翁坐在画面左侧。他靠在右手肘上，右腿伸直，左腿向后弯向座位。他全身赤裸，一件斗篷遮住了一小部分右腿和右臂。右臂抱着两支矛尖指向地面的长矛。他身后的树为他提供着荫蔽。恩底弥翁面向左侧，向下凝视，表示他处于休息的状态。女神塞勒涅从右边姗姗而来，随行的是一位飞翔的爱神。爱神扶住女神的前臂，引导她去恩底弥翁身边。从天而降的女神身体的一部分被飘逸的斗篷覆盖。

Selene and Endymion

Fresco
1st century AD
71cm × 71cm × 8cm

In this fresco from Herculaneum Endymion is seated on the left of the composition, leaning on his right elbow with his right leg extended and his left bent backwards against the seat. He is completely naked except for a cloak that minimally covers his right leg and arm, which holds two spears with the tips pointing to the ground. A tree rising up behind him shelters him and he faces to the left, gaze down, implying he is in a resting state. The goddess Selene, arriving from the right, is accompanied by a flying eros who guides her towards Endymion by holding her forearm. She is partly covered by a cloak, flowing in the wind as she descends from the sky.

勒达

壁画
公元 1 世纪
68.5cm × 57cm × 6.5cm

这幅壁画是在庞贝古城的古代狩猎之家发现的。画面中，勒达呈站姿，戴着头巾，左臂上搭着的黄色长袍覆盖了她的下半身，在身体的周围飘扬。勒达惊讶地抬头看着爱神厄洛斯。爱神盘旋在上方，从双耳细颈瓶中倾泻出金色的雨水。一道雷电（象征着宙斯）斜着出现在画面右侧的岩石上。

Leda

Fresco
1st century AD
68.5cm × 57cm × 6.5cm

This fresco was discovered in the House of the Ancient Hunt in Pompeii and depicts Leda standing, adorned with a headband and holding with her left arm a yellow robe that covers her lower body, flowing around her. She gases upwards in astonishment at Eros, who hovers above while pouring golden rain from an amphora. A thunderbolt leans on a rock on the right side of the composition.

伽倪墨得斯与鹰

大理石
公元 2 世纪
182cm×80cm×51cm

伽倪墨得斯是位年轻的特洛伊王子，被荷马描述为他那个时代最英俊的凡人。众神之王宙斯／朱庇特爱上了他，变成了一只鹰，将他以众神侍酒者的身份带到了奥林匹斯山，并使他长生不老——这可是在他无数的女性情人身上从未发生过的事。

伽倪墨得斯的形象是作为侍酒者或有鹰陪伴的形象传入意大利的，最初被伊特鲁里亚人采用。古罗马帝国时期的众多群雕保存下了他在具象艺术中的形象，其中就有那不勒斯国家考古博物馆藏有的这尊雕塑。作品中，伽倪墨得斯赤裸着身体，懒洋洋地倚靠着旁边的老鹰。

如今，木星（西方文化中称宙斯／朱庇特）的一颗卫星以伽倪墨得斯的名字命名，以纪念他们之间的爱情。

本展品中，年轻的伽倪墨得斯赤身裸体，身材健壮，身体重心放在左腿上。他的右膝弯曲，右脚侧向一边。头略微偏左，头发卷曲。他戴着一顶古希腊时期的弗里吉亚帽。伽倪墨得斯低垂的右臂抱着牧羊人的手杖，左臂则环抱着老鹰。老鹰停在树干上，树干覆盖着斗篷。旁边的狗蹲坐着，抬头望向伽倪墨得斯。

Ganymede and the eagle

Marble
2nd century AD
182cm × 80cm × 51cm

A young Trojan prince, Ganymede is described by Homer as the most handsome of the mortals of his time. The god Zeus/Jupiter fell in love with him and, transformed into an eagle, took him to Olympus in the role of cupbearer of the gods, making him immortal, which never happened with his countless female lovers.

The iconography of the young man arrived in Italy through his figurations as a cupbearer or accompanied by an eagle, initially adopted by the Etruscans. His image in the figurative arts crystallized in the imperial age, through a series of sculptural groups, such as the one now preserved at the Museo Archeologico Nazionale di Napoli, which depict him nude, accompanied by the eagle on which he languidly leans.Today one of the satellites of the planet Jupiter bears his name in tribute to the love affair between them.

Young Ganymede, athletically formed, naked, rests his weight on his left leg. His right leg is bent at the knee and his foot is placed to the side. On his head, which is turned slightly to the left, and on his curly hair, he wears a Phrygian cap. In his lowered right arm he holds the *pedum*, a shepherd's crook, while with his left arm he embraces the eagle, resting on a trunk covered with a cloak. Next to Ganymede is a dog sitting on its hind legs looking up at him.

快意人生：
古罗马人对美好生活的热爱
Life's Pleasures:
The Roman Love for a Good Life

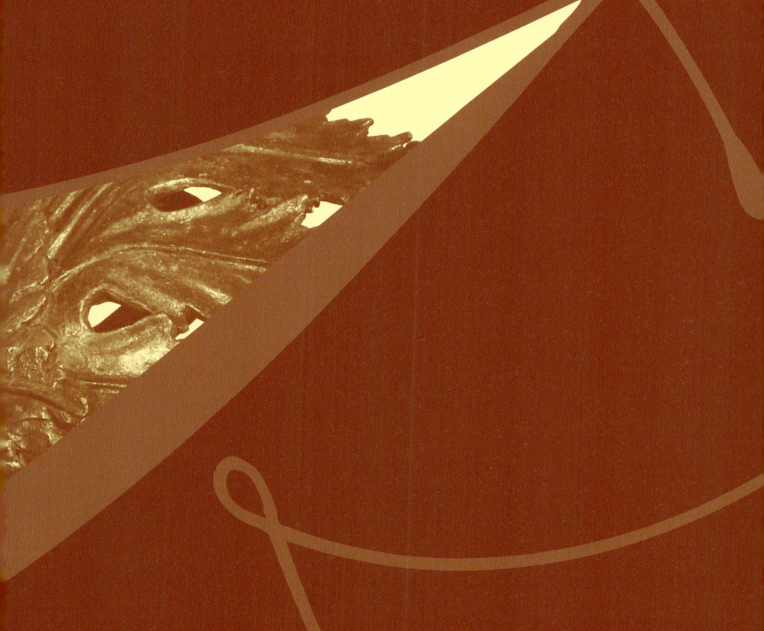

爱，不仅仅关乎激情，更是一种引导人们回归天性的强大力量，它既在天上，更在人间。第三单元所展现的生命力以狄俄尼索斯的形象为代表，展现的是古罗马人对人世间美好生活的热爱。

狄俄尼索斯是古希腊神话中的酒神，奥林匹斯十二主神之一，也是古希腊、古罗马最复杂、最迷人的形象之一。他代表狂喜、热爱与欢乐，在疯狂与睿智、野性与文明的张力中，将雌性和雄性的特质糅合在一起。

他将葡萄藤赐予人类，葡萄串酿成的美酒是古希腊和古罗马人的顶级佳酿。除了酒神的身份，狄俄尼索斯还被认为是戏剧的始祖。古时最初的戏剧表演是酒神节的重要部分，象征着人类的巨大力量。

狄俄尼索斯给人们带来的长远影响渗透在生活的方方面面：美食与美酒带来的乐趣，以及作为聚会欢宴场所的庞贝式住宅和花园展示出的日常生活之美。

Love is not just about the passion, it is a greater force that leads people back to their primordial nature, both in heaven and on earth. The life force in this section is represented by the figure of Dionysus, showing the love of the ancient Romans for the good life on earth.

Dionysus is the god of wine in ancient Greek mythology, one of the twelve main gods of Olympus, and one of the most complex and fascinating figures of ancient Greece and Rome. He represents ecstasy, love and joy, blending female and male qualities in a tension of madness and wisdom, wildness and civilisation.

He bestowed the vine on mankind, and the bunches of grapes made the finest wine of the ancient Greeks and Romans. As well as being the god of wine, Dionysus is also considered to be the inventor of theatre. As the ultimate sign of the representation of humanity, original theatrical performances in ancient times were an integral part of the festivals held in his honour.

The long-lasting influence of Dionysus on people permeated all aspects of life: the food and wine, and the beauty of everyday life through the Pompeian houses and gardens that served as places to gather and feast.

酒神的狂欢：狄俄尼索斯的野性魅力
Dionysus: Charming and Wild

描绘神话故事中神和英雄们爱情的艺术品数不胜数，然而有更多艺术作品呈现了与希腊神话中的酒神和植物之神狄俄尼索斯（罗马神话中称为巴克斯）有关的信仰、神话、思想、仪式和传说，这些内容构成了一个庞大的宗教体系。狄俄尼索斯是古希腊与古罗马文化所设想的最迷人、最复杂的神。其复杂性源于其多面性和难以捉摸但始终存在的特性。这一特征的基础是这位神的"差异性"，即他具有取消事物对立面的能力。的确，狄俄尼索斯将男性与女性、疯狂与智慧、原始与文明结合在一起。

狄俄尼索斯属于地神，是与大地和自然，尤其是和植物有关的神祇，是古希腊人们最信奉的形象之一。根据神话，狄俄尼索斯是众神之王宙斯众多婚外情之一结出的果实。宙斯与忒拜公主塞墨勒孕育狄俄尼索斯后，天后赫拉因宙斯的背叛而震怒，设下计谋，使得塞墨勒在生产前即去世。未足月的狄俄尼索斯被父亲缝在自己的大腿中直到足月，出生后随即被托付给赫耳墨斯。正如古希腊雕刻家普拉克西特列斯创作的著名雕塑群《赫耳墨斯与幼年的狄俄尼索斯》所展示的那样，众神信使赫耳墨斯正带着年幼的狄俄尼索斯到倪萨山，那里的宁芙们后来将狄俄尼索斯抚养长大。

关于倪萨山这座充满水和森林的神山的所在地，最开始有很多种说法，而后被确认为色雷斯。众多学者已证实，与植物神们相关的类似崇拜，正是从色雷斯起源的。这种与大地和季节的关系将狄俄尼索斯与葡萄种植联系在一起，因此当狄俄尼索斯的神话传入意大利时，衍生出了酒神巴克斯。为纪念他而举行的庆祝活动，从乡村节日逐渐转变为真正的神秘仪式。在仪式中，入会者通常是醉酒的女性。她们放纵自己陷入神秘的狂怒之中。这样做的目的，是模拟那些据传说陪伴狄俄尼索斯的萨提尔、小神西勒努斯和女信徒迈那得斯的游行。展现这些人物形象的艺术作品可谓数不胜数，其中最著名的《醉酒的萨提尔》表现的是参加庆祝活动后睡得东倒西歪的萨提尔；另一尊史珂帕斯的雕塑作品《起舞的酒神女信徒》则呈现被狂乱感觉折磨着不停旋转的酒神女信徒。

这种感官知觉的解放是为纪念狄俄尼索斯而举行的仪式的独有特征，正是它使狄俄尼索斯的形象与"活的生命"（Zoè）关联起来。对希腊人来说，这种狂野而不可阻挡的流动代表着"存在"，可以被理解为绝对的、宇宙的、永恒的意义，它不同于"有形式的生命"（Bios），即注定要终止的肉体生命。在当代文化中，这种对神性的看法也被尼采等哲学家沿用。尼采在《悲剧的诞生》中将"酒神的精神"诠释为"日神阿波罗精神"的对立面：前者已成为与非理性生命主义相关的美学范畴；后者则凭借合理有序的理性结构体系成为希腊文化的基础。

这种使狄俄尼索斯势不可挡且富有感染力的狂热，后来以面具作为代表。面具能令人感到不安，也能体现角色难以捉摸的特性。考虑到面具的尺寸和做工，它并非本来就作佩戴之用，而是作为神本身的形象呈现。后来，狄俄尼索斯的形象在艺术中有了多种变化，随之产生这样的肖像画——画中，酒神的头被葡萄藤和葡萄串包围。这样的形象也能在酒神游行中见到，通常描绘在混合水和酒的双柄大口酒罐上。之后，作品中的酒神从古代简洁风格的冷静成年人的形象，过渡到古希腊罗马时期和希腊化时期的愈发少年和慵懒的形象。古希腊罗马时期晚期，酒神的形象被装饰在游行的车头上，庆祝自己凯旋归来。酒神旁边是传说中的妻子阿里阿德涅、克里特岛国王米诺斯的女儿。雅典英雄忒修斯战胜牛头人身怪后，将阿里阿德涅遗弃在纳克索斯岛，阿里阿德涅随后接受了狄俄尼索斯的求婚。

许多画像都描绘了狄俄尼索斯和妻子阿里阿德涅之间充满爱意和幸福的婚姻，他们身处众多萨提尔和酒神女信徒迈那得斯们之间。狄俄尼索斯手中通常捏着的酒杯明确表现着葡萄酒这一标志性元素。由葡萄酒生出的醉意，结合着舞蹈和音乐，带来幸福、爱和狂喜。这样的酒神肖像长期流传，在文艺复兴时期和巴洛克时期被频繁使用。不仅在具象艺术领域，如提香和卡拉奇的作品中出现，而且在文学领域，如洛伦佐·德·美第奇为狂欢节的化装游行队伍写的著名乐歌《酒神巴克斯和仙女阿里阿德涅的胜利》，颂扬了青春的转瞬即逝，呼吁人们像这位希腊神祇和他的新娘一样，纵情恣肆地享受生活的乐趣。

Numerous are the representations of the loves of gods and heroes of myth, but even more numerous are the representations connected with that vast religious complex of cults, myths, ideas, rites and legends that are associated with the figure of Dionysus/Bacchus, god of wine and wilderness. Dionysus is the most fascinating and complex god that Greek and Roman culture has conceived; a complexity that stems from his being multifaceted, elusive but constantly present. Underlying this characteristic is his ability to undo opposites. Dionysus, in fact, combines male and female, madness and wisdom, savage and civilized.

A chthonic deity, linked to the earth and its many manifestations, especially in the sphere of the plant world, Dionysus is one of the most important figures in the religiosity of ancient Greece. The myth concerning his birth sees him as the result of one of Zeus' many adulterous affairs. The father of the gods conceived him with Semele, a Theban princess who, struck by the wrath of the betrayed Hera, perished before giving birth to him. Too premature to survive, Dionysus is sewn by his father into his own thigh, where he ends his gestation time. Once he comes into the light, he is entrusted to Hermes, as shown in Praxiteles' well-known sculpture, *Hermes and the Infant Dionysus*, and taken to the Nymphs of Nysa for them to raise him.

Among the various regions where this mythical place called Nysa, rich in water and forests, was fabled to be located, Thracia has been identified, a land where many scholars have detected the origin of similar cults related to deities connected with the plant world. It is precisely this connection with the land and the seasons that links the god to the cultivation of the vine, so much so that when the myth landed in Italy it gave birth to Bacchus, god of wine. The festivities in his honour would thus gradually transform from rural festivals into authentic mystery rites, in which the initiates, often female and intoxicated with wine, would indulge in a veritable mystical frenzy. This was meant to simulate those processions of satyrs, sileni and maenads that, according to myth, accompanied Dionysus. Numerous in time would be the representations made of these characters. Among the best known are the Barberini Faun, who sleeps discomposedly after participating in one of these events, and the Dancing Maenad by sculptor Skopas, portrayed as she twirls in sensual delirium.

It is precisely this liberation of the senses, a peculiar feature of the rites in his honour, that makes Dionysus a figure linked to creation understood as "Zoè", that wild and unstoppable flowing that for the Greeks represented existence understood in an absolute, cosmic, eternal sense, distinct from "Bios", the life of the physical body that was, instead, destined to cease. Such a vision of divinity would be taken up in contemporary culture by philosophers such as Nietzsche, who, in *The Birth of Tragedy*, contrasts the "Dionysian," which has become a true aesthetic category linked to an irrational vitalism, with the "Apollonian," that system of rational and ordered constructions that underlies Greek culture.

This frenzy that makes Dionysus unstoppable and fluid will begin to be symbolized by a mask, a perturbing object capable of narrating the character's elusiveness, so much so that it is not born to be worn, given its size and workmanship, but to be the very image of the deity. The latter will be declined in the arts in various ways, giving rise to iconographies that see the god with his head girded with vines and grape bunches, but also engaged in the convulsive processions associated with his myth, often depicted on kraters, typical wide-mouthed vessels born to mix water with wine. The modes of representation concerning him will move from the more composed and adult images of the archaic and severe period, to the gradually more childlike and indolent ones of the classical and Hellenistic periods, which will be followed, in the late antique period, by those that see him driving a chariot, in the act of celebrating his own triumph, next to his mythical consort Ariadne, who, daughter of Minos, offers herself to him in marriage after being abandoned by Theseus on his return from his victorious expedition on the Minotaur.

There are numerous images that portray him next to his bride Ariadne in a loving and joyous union between satyrs and maenads: wine, which he clasps in his hands, remains his defining element, the instrument of intoxication that leads to happiness, love and ecstasy achieved through dancing and music. This iconographic theme would survive for a long time, becoming frequently adopted during the Renaissance and Baroque not only in the figurative field, as in the case of works such as those by Titian and Carracci, but also in the literary field, as in Lorenzo the Magnificent's famous song *Triumph of Bacchus*, where the fleeting nature of youth is exalted and the invitation is given to abandon oneself to the joys of life just like the Greek God and his bride.

有酒神醉酒图案的双柱形柄大口罐

陶
公元前 5 世纪
51cm × 45cm

这种大口罐是公元前 7 世纪最后 25 年在古希腊城邦科林斯发明的。它从几何形的大口罐发展而来，在古代似乎被称为科林斯大口罐。罐身为球形，有双层矮足，罐颈较宽，口沿平而凸出。罐的名称来源于其手柄的垂直的圆柱形状。双柄从罐身开始伸展，与罐口边缘连接，高度又不超过罐口。这件展品上装饰着与酒神狄俄尼索斯有关的人物形象。

Column krater with Dionysus inebriated

Pottery
5th century BC
51cm × 45cm

Invented in Corinth in the last quarter of the 7th century BC, the column krater developed from the geometric krater and seems to have been known in antiquity as the Corinthian krater; it has a globular body, a short, double-stepped foot, a wide neck and a flat, projecting rim. The handles, whose shape gave the type its name, consist of two vertical cylindrical elements that start from the body and join above the shaped projection of the rim, without exceeding it in height. The decoration represents red figures related to the god Dionysus.

有酒神与酒神游行图案的钟形双柄大口罐

陶
公元前 5 世纪
32cm × 35cm

这种大口罐可以追溯到公元前 5 世纪初，是那个时期红绘图案大口罐的一种变体。罐的形状像一口倒过来的钟，口沿外扩，足矮柄短，罐身上部有两个小横柄。这件展品一并展示了仪式中的狄俄尼索斯与陪伴他的人物，是非常特别的装饰图案。

Bell krater with Dionysus and his court

Pottery
5th century BC
32cm × 35cm

This krater is a variant that originated in the red figure period, at the beginning of the 5th century BC. It is in the shape of an inverted bell and has a flared rim, raised on a foot with a short stem and has two small upturned handles at the top of the body. Very particular is this decoration that shows Dionysus together with the figures accompanying him at ritual moments.

有酒神游行图案的双柄大口高脚杯

陶

公元前 5 世纪

37cm × 34cm

这种高脚杯从公元前 6 世纪下半叶流传开
来，在红绘人物时期变得非常流行。杯身
高大外展，有时呈凸形如花萼。杯身下部
镶有微斜的小手柄。高脚呈双层。这件展
品黑色的背景上，狄俄尼索斯和他的游行
队伍以红色的形象呈现。

Calyx krater with Dionysian procession

Pottery

5th century BC

37cm × 34cm

This type of vase became widespread from the second half
of the 6th century BC onwards but became very popular in
the red-figure period. It has a tall, flared body, sometimes
with a convex profile like the calyx of a flower from which it
derives its name; the small, slightly oblique handles are set in
the lower part of the body. The foot is elongated and double-
stepped. Dionysus and his procession are represented here in
red figures on a black background.

宝座上的酒神

壁画
公元 1 世纪
89.5cm × 75.5cm × 9cm

本展品为灰泥墙面壁画，属于庞贝第三风格，即装饰风格。它展现的是酒神狄俄尼索斯的形象。酒神坐在宝座上，穿着古罗马凉鞋。他的右脚放在脚踏上，左脚向内弯曲。酒神的披风盖住了身体的一小部分，从左肩滑下，覆在大腿上。他的胸前围着祭祀羔羊的薄羊皮。宝座有刻着浮雕的座腿，靠背为长方形，放置在一根柱子前。酒神的右手放在宝座扶手上，手中拿着他最爱的大酒杯。酒杯被绘制成黄色，意味着它是用黄金做的。酒神的左手挂着酒神杖，手杖顶部装饰有饰带和植物。观者左手边的地板上有一只用于纪念酒神的仪式的鼓，右边有一只豹子，它是酒神的神兽。

Dionysus on the throne

Fresco
1st century AD
89.5cm × 75.5cm × 9cm

Frescoed wall plaster pertaining to the third Pompeian style. The god Dionysus is depicted: seated on a throne, he rests his right foot, clad in a sandal, forward on a shaped footrest, while his left foot, also clad, is placed backwards. His mantle leaves most of his body bare, hanging from his left shoulder and draped over his thighs. The god's chest is girded with a thin nebris, the skin of a sacrificed fawn. The throne has carved legs, a rectangular back, and is placed in front of a column. With his right hand, lowered onto the armrest of the throne, the god holds a kantharos, his favourite vessel, painted in yellow to signify gold. His raised left hand holds the thyrsus: a staff adorned with ribbons and a plant tuft at the top. To the left of the beholder, on the floor, is a tambourine, used during ceremonies in honour of Dionysus; to the right is a panther, an animal sacred to the god.

起舞的酒神女信徒

壁画
公元 1 世纪
74cm × 60cm × 7cm

本展品是灰泥墙面壁画，属于庞贝第三风
格，即装饰风格。黑色背景下呈现的是女信
徒迈那得斯的形象。她是酒神队列的一员，朝
着观者右手边的方向飞翔。迈那得斯穿着一
件轻盈得几乎透明的及脚长衫，上身覆盖着
薄纱，头戴花冠。伸出的左手执酒神杖，向
身后垂下的右手拿着一只鼓。

Dancing maenad

Fresco
1st century AD
74cm × 60cm × 7cm

Frescoed wall plaster pertaining to the third Pompeian style.
On a black background is depicted a maenad, a character
from Bacchus' procession, flying towards the right of the
viewer. The maenad wears a light, almost transparent, foot-
length dress completed by a veil covering her torso and her
head is crowned with flowers. In her left hand she holds the
stem of a thyrsus, while in her lowered right hand she holds
a tambourine.

起舞的酒神女信徒

壁画
公元 1 世纪
36.5cm × 25.5cm × 5cm

这幅公元 1 世纪的壁画来自庞贝古城，描
绘的是一位跳舞的酒神女信徒。酒神女信
徒是与酒神狄俄尼索斯相关狂欢仪式的
典型人物。其名字在古希腊语中的字面意
思是"发疯"，也就是说，它表明女性处于
生命之神狄俄尼索斯引发的狂喜中。

Dancing maenad

Fresco
1st century AD
36.5cm × 25.5cm × 5cm

A 1st century AD fresco from Pompeii,
depicting a maenad dancing. The
maenad is a typical figure in orgiastic
rites connected to Dionysus. The name
in ancient Greek literally translates to
"being mad". It thus indicates women
in the grip of ecstatic frenzy induced by
Dionysus, god of the life force.

绘有情爱场面的墙壁

壁画
公元 1 世纪
215cm × 182cm × 12cm

这件展品为带有黑色和红色几何形状的庞贝墙壁上的典型建筑装饰。墙壁中央的正方形里描绘着情爱场面的图案。

Wall fragment with erotic scene

Fresco
1st century AD
215cm × 182cm × 12cm

Typical Pompeian architectural wall decoration with geometric partition in black and red. In the panel at the center of the wall is depicted an erotic subject.

青年酒神头像

大理石
公元 2 世纪
64cm × 45cm × 45cm

这尊头微微前倾的半身像呈现的是年轻时的
酒神狄俄尼索斯。作品中，酒神的脸庞柔软
光滑、浓密的卷发一直垂到肩部。酒神的这
种形象可以追溯到公元前 4 世纪中叶。

Colossal head of young Dionysus

Marble
2nd century AD
64cm × 45cm × 45cm

With his head slightly bent forward, this
bust is a depiction of the god Dionysus at
a young age. The face with its soft, smooth
surfaces is framed by a thick mass of curly
hair that descends to the attachment of
the shoulders. The iconographic model of
this representation of Dionysus dates back
to the mid-4th century BC.

萨提尔雕像

青铜
公元 1 世纪
15cm × 6cm

这座青铜小雕像呈现的是舞动的萨提尔。人物正在旋转中，左腿前伸，脚尖点地，右腿后撤，也以脚尖着地。萨提尔的双臂同时抬起，左臂伸向脸颊，右臂弯曲高举，生殖器膨出。整座雕像放置在一个圆形底座上。

Satyr figurine

Bronze
1st century AD
15cm × 6cm

Bronze figurine depicting a dancing satyr. The figure is depicted in a rotating movement, with the left leg advanced and the foot resting on the ground with the toes only, just as the right leg is set back and the foot is likewise resting on the ground with the toes only. Symmetrically, the arms are raised and advanced, the left turned towards the face, the right curved with the hand raised. The sexual organ is swollen. The figurine is placed on a circular shaped base.

有情爱场面的灯具

赤陶
公元 1 世纪
4cm × 8cm × 11cm

这盏油灯带有圆形槽及涡形灯嘴。圆盘边缘有多条同心凹槽，中间刻画的是一对男女在一张矮床腿、高床垫的床上前后位结合的画面。圆盘中有一个小孔，用于注入灯油。灯嘴上有燃烧物的痕迹。

Oil lamp with erotic scene

Terracotta
1st century AD
4cm × 8cm × 11cm

Oil-lamp with circular bowl and voluted nozzle. The shoulder is marked by a series of concentric grooves that enclose a figurative scene: a heterosexual couple, intent on sexual intercourse from behind, is on a bed on low turned legs with a high mattress. In the disc is a small oil-hole, while the nozzle hole shows remnants of burning.

有情爱场面的灯具

赤陶
公元 1 世纪
5cm × 6cm × 12cm

这盏油灯带有圆形槽、涡形灯嘴及环状把手。圆盘边缘的多条同心凹槽，中央的场景描绘的是一对躺在床上的男女。他们的身体被床单缠绕，意图从背后结合。圆盘上有一个小油孔，灯嘴有部分损坏。

Oil lamp with erotic scene

Terracotta
1st century AD
5cm × 6cm × 12cm

Oil-lamp with circular bowl, volutes on the nozzle and a ring shaped handle. The shoulder is marked by concentric grooves that enclose a scene with two lovers. The scene depicts a heterosexual couple intent on sexual intercourse from behind lying on a bed and intertwined in the sheets. In the disc is a small oil-hole while the nozzle is partly broken.

萨提尔雕像

大理石
公元 1 世纪
178cm × 73cm × 37cm

这是一尊雕工精美的萨提尔休息像。萨提尔是生活在树林和高山中的神话人物，象征着大自然的活力和力量，与酒神崇拜一脉相连。早期呈半人半羊形象，长着带络腮胡子的人脸以及山羊的犄角、尾巴和腿脚。而随着时间推移，萨提尔的形象逐渐失去了动物特征。这尊雕像正是如此，在对人体的塑造中糅合了造型与尺寸的优雅。

Statue of a satyr

Marble
1st century AD
178cm × 73cm × 37cm

A depiction of a satyr in a resting state. The satyr is a mythological figure that inhabits woods and mountains, personifies the vitality and strength of nature and is connected with the Dionysian cult. Depicted at first as a mixture of bearded human appearance and animal characteristics such as horns, tail and goat's feet, he has lost some of his animal attributes over time. This is the case in this depiction where the paleness of the body is combined with the elegance of its form and size.

奢华与休闲
Luxury and Relaxation

长期以来，古罗马人用餐的地方相当简朴，家具也仅限于必需品。然而，在公元前 3 世纪和公元前 2 世纪之间，富裕的罗马家庭的住宅不断扩大，越来越多的空间用于会客和起居。

在具有纪念意义的房屋中，卧躺餐厅尤为重要。那里，人们躺在欢宴床上用餐。这些床以马蹄形布置在桌子周围，铺放着舒适的垫子和毯子，人们可以舒适地躺在上面，将上半身靠在左边。

在会客厅里，富裕的家庭可以接待客人并放松身心。客厅四周布置着奢华而贵重的物品，人们普遍用较大的雕像、挂毯、壁画和马赛克来装饰环境。这些房间还配有桌子、长凳、烛台、火炉和火盆。为了强调奢华和放松的气氛，奴隶们在油灯中加入香精，用异国情调的气味取悦食客。

For a long time, the place where ancient Romans ate meals had been rather austere with furniture limited to the essentials. However, between the third and second centuries B.C., the dwellings of wealthy Roman families expanded, and more and more space was allocated to spaces of representation and living rooms.

In monumental houses, special importance is given to the dining room, the triclinium, where people ate while lying on *klinai* (convivial beds) arranged in a horseshoe shape around a table. They were made comfortable by pillows and blankets, on which one could lie comfortably, resting on one's left side.

In the spaces of representation, reception rooms, wealthy families could receive guests and relax, surrounded by luxurious and valuable objects. It was the tendency to decorate the room by embellishing it with statues, wall hangings, frescoes and mosaics, often of large dimensions. These rooms were also furnished with tables, stools, candelabra, stoves and braziers. To increase the atmosphere of luxury and relaxation, slaves added scented essences to oil lamps, delighting diners with exotic scents.

精巧的建筑

壁画
公元 1 世纪
73.5cm × 80.5cm × 7cm

本展品是庞贝古城的壁画墙饰，所绘内容为建筑，具有视觉上的错觉效果。

Fantastical architecture

Fresco
1st century AD
73.5cm × 80.5cm × 7cm

Frescoed wall decoration from Pompeii with architectural subject matter and illusionistic effect.

精巧的建筑

壁画
公元 1 世纪
121cm × 96.5cm × 10.5cm

本展品是庞贝古城的壁画墙饰，所绘内容为建筑，具有视觉上的错觉效果。

Fantastical architecture

Fresco
1st century AD
121cm × 96.5cm × 10.5cm

Frescoed wall decoration from Pompeii with architectural subject matter and illusionistic effect.

诗人与建筑

壁画
公元 1 世纪
83cm × 80cm × 5cm

本展品是庞贝古城的壁画墙饰，所绘内容为建筑，具有视觉上的错觉效果。这件作品中绘有一张戏剧面具和一位诗人的形象。

Poet and architecture

Fresco
1st century AD
83cm × 80cm × 5cm

Frescoed wall decoration from Pompeii with architectural subject matter and illusionistic effect with the presence of a theatre mask and the figure of a poet.

古罗马人的宴会
The Banquet

奢华也在宴会等"特殊场合"中得到展现和强调。宴会是社交和政治互动的重要场合，巩固着亲属关系、从属关系或对主人的依赖关系。

古罗马的宴会是知识分子的社交场合，音乐和表演为宴会带来欢乐的气氛。食物也不再仅限于食用价值，而更是成为展示优雅和奢华的手段，代表着个人的社会地位。食物与美酒、音乐、歌唱、交谈和游戏一起，放大着快乐，营造出享受和炫耀的氛围。

从维苏威火山地区壁画常描绘的欢乐场景中，我们能够感受到庞贝式的宴会的生动氛围。宴会厅前的客厅中常装饰着描绘戏剧场景的小画，似乎为我们暗示着当时穿插于宴会中的精彩表演。静物主题的小画中则关注烹饪的美食和大地作物的美味，画中反复描绘着鱼、野味、蔬菜和水果。

Luxury also found its manifestation and exaltation in special occasions, such as banquets. These were important occasions of social and political interaction, during which ties of kinship, affiliation or dependence on the master of the house were consolidated.

The Roman banquet is a social and intellectual gathering, enlivened by music and entertainment, during which food becomes the pretext for exhibiting refinement and luxury, as manifestations of one's social status. Food, accompanied by wine and music, singing, conversation, and games, becomes an exaltation of pleasures, an occasion for enjoyment and ostentation.

The atmosphere of the Pompeian banquets is still alive in the frequent scenes found in the paintings. Often in the rooms preceding the banquet room, small paintings appear with theatrical scenes, which seem to allude to the performances that were held during the banquets. In the still life paintings, attention to the delicacies of the kitchen and the taste of the products of the earth appear: depictions of fish, game, vegetables and fruit are recurrent.

有面具图案的浮雕

大理石
公元 1 世纪
26cm × 33cm × 5cm

本展品是一张刻有戏剧人物面具的大理石板。左右两侧以高浮雕手法刻画了两张面具；第三张刻在下层；位于左侧面具之后的第四张面具以浅浮雕手法刻画。右侧的男性喜剧人物面具，特征为下巴的短胡须和脸上沟壑般的皱纹。左侧的年轻女性人物面具后面，以浅浮雕手法刻画了一个前额头发竖起的人物侧脸。下部的面具呈悲剧人物形象，特点是一绺一绺的长胡须。在古典时代，戏剧演出是最普遍的社会活动之一。

Relief with masks

Marble
1st century AD
26cm × 33cm × 5cm

Marble slab with theatre masks. Represented in high relief are two masks placed vertically at the two side ends, a third placed on the base and a fourth in lower relief behind the mask on the left. On the right is a male comedic mask, characterised by a short beard on the chin and wrinkles furrowing the face. On the left is that of a young female figure, behind which can be seen, in lower relief, the outline of a face characterised by hair raised on the forehead. At the bottom is a tragical mask, characterised by a long beard with parted curls. Theatrical performances were among the most popular social events of antiquity.

有宴会图案的双耳瓶

陶
公元前 6 世纪
37cm × 27cm

这种双耳瓶用于运输或存放液体。罐身宴
会场景的绘制采用了比红绘更古老的原始
黑绘技法。

Amphora with banquet scene

Pottery
6th century BC
37cm × 27cm

Large vase with two handles used to carry or
contain liquids. The banquet representation is
made using the black-figure technique, which is
older in origin than the red-figure technique.

有宴会图案的双柱形柄大口罐

陶

公元前 5 世纪

37cm × 34cm

这件大口罐因罐子两侧的两个柱形的手柄得名。上面以红色描绘了带有人物的宴会场景。用餐者们斜倚在两张桌子旁边的两张长榻上。中间的人正在弹奏古希腊的七弦琴，右边的人正在用高脚杯喝水。带有此类图案的大口罐是了解宴会在古代社会中的作用以及酒的重要性的主要途径。

Column krater with banquet scene

Pottery

5th century BC

37cm × 34cm

This column krater was given its name by the set of two vertical handles located on either side. It features a banquet scene with red-figures; diners are reclining on two couches beside two tables. The figure in the centre is playing the lyre, while the figure to the right is drinking from a kylix cup. Examples with such depictions can be used as a primary source to understand the role of banquets in ancient society and the importance of wine.

有宴会图案的钟形双柄大口罐

Bell krater with banquet scene

陶
公元前 4 世纪
40cm × 39cm

Pottery
4th century BC
40cm × 39cm

双柄大口罐是古希腊和古罗马容器中最容易识别其
形状的容器之一。通常在酒会中放在房间中央最显
眼的位置。它是一种用来混合酒和水的开口大罐。
这件展品描绘的是宴会场景，其中用红色精细描绘
了三个斜倚着的人物形象以及一个站立的人物形象。

The krater is one of the most identifiable shapes in
the ancient Greek and Roman catalogue of vessels.
Usually placed prominently in the centre of the room
at a symposium, it was a large, open-mouthed bowl
used for mixing wine with water. This example shows
a banquet scene with three highly detailed reclining
red-figures and one standing.

有面具图案的舞台布景

壁画
公元 1 世纪
71cm × 102.5cm × 9cm

该展品为灰泥壁画，属于庞贝第三风格，即装饰风格。画面中绘有两根支撑门楣的柱子，柱子中间有一张放在阶梯上的悲剧人物面具。从观者的角度看，面具侧向左边。面具展示的是一个戏剧女主角的面庞。柱子和门楣之间绘有水果垂饰，上面有每三只为一串的苹果。

Theatrical scene with mask

Fresco
1st century AD
71cm × 102.5cm × 9cm

Frescoed wall plaster pertaining to the third Pompeian style. Framed between two shaped pillars supporting an architrave is a tragic mask resting on some steps. The mask, turned to the viewer's left, represents the face of a female dramatic protagonist. From the pillars and the architrave hangs a vegetal festoon, in which apples are arranged in groups of three.

有面具图案的舞台布景

壁画
公元 1 世纪
72.5cm × 104.5cm × 9.5cm

该展品为灰泥壁画，属于庞贝第三风格，即装饰风格。画面与前一幅作品非常相似，是一张放在阶梯上的悲剧人物面具。面具表现的是年迈的人物形象，在正剧和喜剧中都很常见。环绕整个画面的垂饰上绘有三只一串的苹果（除了右下角的那一串是两只苹果）。苹果垂饰之间间隔着角状玻璃酒器、芦苇排箫、鼓和一个带提手的玻璃盘。

Theatrical scene with mask

Fresco
1st century AD
72.5cm × 104.5cm × 9.5cm

Frescoed wall plaster pertaining to the third Pompeian style. With a framing quite similar to that of the previous work is a tragic mask, facing to the right of the viewer, resting on some steps. The mask represents the face of an old man, frequent in both dramatic and comedic representations. The plant festoon surrounding the scene shows apples in groups of three (except in the lower groups, in which there are two) interspersed with glass horns, used for drinking; a pan flute made of reeds; a tambourine; and a glass dish with a raised handle.

有葡萄串和山鹑的静物

壁画
公元 1 世纪
30cm × 29cm × 6cm

这幅壁画是小幅静物画，绘于灰泥墙面。从观者角度来看，棕色背景上有一只面对左侧的鸟，它的面前是一串带有葡萄叶的葡萄。

Still life with grapes and partridge

Fresco
1st century AD
30cm × 29cm × 6cm

Frescoed painting on wall plaster representing a 'still life'. On an undifferentiated brown background there is a recumbent bird facing towards the left of the viewer in front of a rich bunch of grapes, complete with a few leaves.

有无花果的静物

壁画
公元 1 世纪
38cm×55.5cm×5cm

这幅彩绘灰泥墙面壁画，是一幅绘有无花果与桃子的"静物画"。前景绘画了一个平台，五个挂在带叶树枝上的无花果位于观者右侧位置。而观者左侧位置则有三个桃子，其中一个放在平台上，另外两个悬挂在画面左上角。整个画面以棕色为背景。

Still life with figs

Fresco
1st century AD
38cm × 55.5cm × 5cm

Painted wall plaster representing a "still life" with figs and peaches. A ledge is in the foreground on which five figs are resting to the right of the viewer, hanging from a branch with leaves. To the left of the viewer are three peaches, one resting on the ledge and two hanging from the upper left corner. The whole scene is set on a brown background.

有鱼的静物

壁画
公元 1 世纪
36cm × 79.5cm × 6cm

在代表着水的蓝色背景上，绘画了六条不同种类的
鱼和一只蛤蜊，壁画的底部和右侧包围着红色边框。
右下角有一段小小的白色柱子。

Still life with fish

Fresco
1st century AD
36cm × 79.5cm × 6cm

Six fishes of various types and one clam can be
seen depicted on a blue background, representing
water, enclosed by a red border at the bottom and
right side of the fresco. A small white column sits
on the bottom right corner.

有无花果的静物

壁画
公元 1 世纪
23cm×41cm×6cm

画面上的水果至少有五个无花果，分两层摆放。两
层搁板和水果的阴影令画面产生了纵深感。无花果
是古罗马人普遍食用的水果，时常被绘画于壁画中。

Still life with figs

Fresco
1st century AD
23cm × 41cm × 6cm

Fruit, of which at least five figs, are depicted on
two levels. The two ledges and the shadows of
the fruits create depth in the painting. Figs were
a common fruit eaten by the ancient Romans and
are often found depicted on frescoes.

餐具
Tableware

古罗马人餐桌上使用的器具是由多种多样的材料制成的：从最不起眼的陶土，到玻璃，再到最珍贵的青铜和银，它们都见证着主人不同层次的财富水平。

餐桌用具包括用于盛放固体食物的容器和盛装、倾倒或饮用液体的容器。食物放在大盘子里，每位用餐者使用较小的容器（例如不同形状的杯子和碗）来盛装自己食用的部分。当时人们用餐时主要使用勺子，而餐叉的使用则未经证实。

葡萄酒用具包括双耳细颈瓶、双柄大口酒罐、用来混合酒（当时的酒是要经过调配才喝的）和舀酒的勺子、用来倒酒的酒罐、用来喝酒的高脚杯和玻璃杯、用来过滤酒的过滤器。具有古希腊风格的形状优雅的器皿，即所谓的茶炊，冬天可用来加热水，夏天则可以填加雪，并将雪压实，用以冷却葡萄酒。

The tablewares of the ancient Romans were made of the most diverse materials: from the humblest clay, to glass and the most valuable bronze and silver, testifying to the different levels of wealth of the owner.

Table service consisted of vessels intended for solid foods and those for holding, pouring, or drinking liquids. Food was presented in large serving dishes, from which each diner served themselves using smaller containers, such as cups and small bowls. The only cutlery was the spoon, while the use of a fork is not attested.

Wine service included amphorae, kraters for wine, ladles for mixing (wine was not drunk pure) and drawing it, pitchers for pouring it, cups and glasses for drinking, and strainers for filtering it. Elegantly shaped vessels of Hellenistic derivation, the so-called samovars, were used in winter to heat water, while in summer wine could be cooled with snow.

鹿头形来通杯

青铜
公元 1 世纪
直径 14cm

本展品为青铜鹿头形来通杯。这种容器有盛酒的功能，在宴会中有专门的支架来摆放它。这种杯子的形状从动物的角衍生而来，因而当时这类容器普遍使用动物头的形状。比如这件容器就采用了鹿头的造型。它的特点是分叉的鹿角和细长的耳朵。这件青铜鹿头形来通杯的顶部有串珠形的饰带。

Deer-head Rhyton

Bronze
1st century AD
Diameter 14cm

Bronze rhyton in the shape of a deer head. The vessel had the function of containing wine, and was used, by means of special supports, during banquets. The representation of animal heads is, given the general shape of this type of vessel derived from that of the horn, very widespread. In this case we have a deer head, characterised by its branched horns and long, thin ears. The upper rim of the rhyton is marked by an astragal frieze.

酒袋壶

青铜
公元 1 世纪
19cm × 10cm × 20cm

酒袋壶是一种古希腊瓶，用于倾倒少量油性液
体，例如将油倒入油灯。它有几种带有动物或
人的造型的变体，材质为陶瓷和青铜。这件青
铜酒袋壶有着制作精美的抽象造型，特点是其
非常优雅的丝状手柄。

Askos

Bronze
1st century AD
19cm × 10cm × 20cm

The askos is an ancient Greek form of vase used for
pouring small quantities of oily liquids, for example to
fill oil lamps. There are several variants of it, zoomorphic
or anthropomorphic, in ceramic and bronze. This one, in
bronze, has a beautifully crafted abstract shape and is
characterised by a very elegant filiform handle.

过滤勺

青铜
公元 1 世纪
4cm × 31cm × 8cm

这支过滤勺，或者更确切地说是过滤器，是酿造和饮用葡萄酒的必备配件，因为当时的人们会用它来过滤葡萄酒中的沉淀物，使得葡萄酒便于饮用。

Colander

Bronze
1st century AD
4cm × 31cm × 8cm

This colander, or better described as a strainer, was an essential accessory for the making and drinking of wine, as it would have been used to filter sediment from wine in order to drink it.

高卢南部红精陶盏

陶
公元 1 世纪
13cm × 25cm

红精陶是一种亮红色、经过抛光的陶，通常也称为萨米亚陶，公元前 1 世纪到公元 3 世纪间在整个罗马帝国普遍被使用。红精陶器上常带有图案和陶器制造者的印记。陶器的风格随时间推移而变化，而制造者的标记则是判断制造年代的重要手段。红精陶器通常被认为是最美丽的陶器类型，是豪华宴会上必要的点睛之物。

South Gaulish terra sigillata cup

Pottery
1st century AD
13cm × 25cm

Terra sigillata is a bright red polished pottery, often also called Samian ware, used throughout the Roman Empire from the 1st century BC to the 3rd century AD. It is often impressed with designs and pottery maker stamps. The fluctuation of the styles over time and the potter's mark provide valuable means for their dating. It is generally considered the most beautiful type of pottery, a necessary addition to luxurious banquets.

高卢南部红精陶盏

陶
公元 1 世纪
7cm × 14cm

这件红精陶盏的底部呈喇叭状，装饰图案中，可能为莨苕花的阔叶及天马珀伽索斯的形象交替出现。这件红精陶盏的形状和装饰均用模具制成。

South Gaulish terra sigillata cup

Pottery
1st century AD
7cm × 14cm

The lower part of the cup, flared in shape, is richly decorated with what seems to be large leaves of Acanthus mollis, alternated with the image of Pegasus. The terra sigillata vessel forms and decorations were made through the use of a mould.

红精陶盘

陶
公元 1 世纪
5cm × 18cm

Terra sigillata plate

Pottery
1st century AD
5cm × 18cm

红精陶盘

陶
公元 1 世纪
5cm × 19cm

Terra sigillata plate

Pottery
1st century AD
5cm × 19cm

古意大利红精陶杯

陶
公元 1 世纪
14cm × 18cm

Italic terra sigillata cup

Pottery
1st century AD
14cm × 18cm

古意大利红精陶杯

陶
公元 1 世纪
14cm × 19cm

Italic terra sigillata cup

Pottery
1st century AD
14cm × 19cm

红精陶小水壶

陶
公元 1 世纪
直径 12cm

这是一把圆形陶水壶。圆形壶体上伸出一个高高的圆柱形壶颈，张开的壶口边缘装饰以线条。从壶肩到壶颈的上端有一根带状柄，在高处弯折。壶面整体光滑。

Terra sigillata jug

Pottery
1st century AD
Diameter 12cm

Spheroidal jug in terra sigillata pottery. From the body rises a tall cylindrical neck with an expanded rim. From the shoulder of the body to the upper part of the neck there is a ribbon-like handle, angled at the top. The surface is uniformly smooth.

竖棱杯

玻璃
公元 1 世纪
19cm × 10cm

Ribbed drinking glass

Glass
1st century AD
19cm × 10cm

竖棱杯

玻璃
公元 1 世纪
17cm × 10cm

Ribbed drinking glass

Glass
1st century AD
17cm × 10cm

092

竖棱碗

玻璃
公元 1 世纪
7cm × 14cm

Ribbed bowl

Glass
1st century AD
7cm × 14cm

餐桌用水罐

玻璃
公元 1 世纪
9cm × 10cm

这是一把绿色的玻璃小水罐。罐身为球形，罐底较平。短的罐颈边缘加粗、刻有纹路并呈喇叭状张开。耳柄由两根细长杆构成，从罐身最宽处延伸至罐沿。罐沿上，耳柄端头的两侧各延伸出五个圆形凸起装饰，上部有一个斜向上挑起的把手，用大拇指扣住它可以更方便地使用水罐。

Glass Pitcher

Glass
1st century AD
9cm × 10cm

Green-coloured glass jug. Spherical body on small flat base. Short hollowed neck with enlarged and grooved rim, flared externally. The handle, in the form of a double rod, runs from the full circumference of the body to the rim. On the latter, it is surrounded by a series of five outgrowths of circular shape on each side. Above is an oblique raised element, used as a thumb-rest to facilitate the use of the jug.

酒袋壶

玻璃
公元 1 世纪
11cm × 12cm × 6cm

Askos

Glass
1st century AD
11cm × 12cm × 6cm

仿大理石小杯

陶
公元 1 世纪
13cm × 6cm

Marble-like cup

Pottery
1st century AD
13cm × 6cm

盛装酱汁的仿大理石小杯

陶
公元 1 世纪
4cm×6cm

Marble-like cup for sauces

Pottery
1st century AD
4cm × 6cm

盛装酱汁的仿大理石小杯

陶
公元 1 世纪
4cm×7cm

Marble-like cup for sauces

Pottery
1st century AD
4cm × 7cm

勺子

银
公元 1 世纪
12cm × 5cm

Spoon

Silver
1st century AD
12cm × 5cm

勺子

银
公元 1 世纪
8cm × 4cm

带梨形勺头的银质针柄勺。勺柄开
始和末端装饰着凹槽和珠子。这种
形状较大的勺子很可能用于食用汤
或粥。

Spoon

Silver
1st century AD
8cm × 4cm

A silver cochlear spoon with a
pear-shaped bowl. The handle is
decorated with grooves and beads
along the beginning and end of
the shaft. These larger shaped
spoons would have most likely
been used for soup or porridge.

小勺

青铜
公元 1 世纪
12cm × 3cm

这是一柄带有圆形勺头的小勺。这种小勺子可能
用于食用鸡蛋、贝类和蜗牛。

Teaspoon

Bronze
1st century AD
12cm × 3cm

Small spoon with a round shaped bowl. These
smaller spoons would have been used for eating
eggs, shellfish and snails.

小勺

银
公元 1 世纪
13cm × 4cm

这是一柄带有圆形勺头的银质小勺。勺柄
形似鼠尾，逐渐收细，末端如针尖。

Teaspoon

Silver
1st century AD
13cm × 4cm

A small silver spoon with a round shaped
bowl. It has a rat-tail like handle that
tapers and ends in a point.

茶炊

青铜
公元 1 世纪
44cm × 37cm

茶炊是一种用于加热液体或使液体保温的容器。容器中空部分的木炭可以加热双层壁内的液体，然后可以从器体上的小孔倒出。本展品有三条动物形状的腿和两个有涡形装饰的手柄。

Samovar

Bronze
1st century AD
44cm × 37cm

A samovar, or autepsa, was a vessel used for heating liquids or keeping them warm. Charcoal in the hollow centre of the vessel would heat the liquid within the double wall. It could then be poured from the small hole found on the body. This example has three animal shaped legs and two handles decorated with volutes.

有面具图案的灯具

青铜
公元 1 世纪
18cm × 12cm

这是一盏青铜材质的油灯，弧形的手柄末
端装饰着一张戏剧面具。

Oil lamp with mask

Bronze
1st century AD
18cm × 12cm

A bronze oil lamp with a theatrical mask
at the end of the curved handle.

有叶状反射物的灯具

青铜
公元 1 世纪
28cm × 40cm × 25cm

这盏油灯有两个涡形灯嘴和一个凹陷的注油孔，注油孔四周环绕着同心圆图案。整个灯身置于一只展开的灯足上。本展品的标志性特征是其很大的手柄。手柄位于灯身的背面，上面的图案是一张美丽的藤叶。

Oil lamp with leaf reflector

Bronze
1st century AD
28cm × 40cm × 25cm

The oil lamp has two volute nozzles and a sunken filling hole with concentric circles surrounding it. The entire body perches on a small, flared foot. The defining feature is a large handle to the back of the body on which rests a beautiful vine leaf motif.

悬挂式三孔灯

青铜
公元 1 世纪
60cm × 35cm × 35cm

这盏青铜油灯侧面有三个灯嘴。灯身上有四根链
条，每个灯嘴上链接着其中的一根，另外一根连
着灯身中央，因而这盏灯可以悬挂在天花板上。
灯足较短，呈圆形。灯身装饰有三个带翼的人头像。

Hanging oil lamp

Bronze
1st century AD
60cm × 35cm × 35cm

A bronze oil lamp with a trio of nozzles projecting from
its sides. Four chains, one on each nozzle and one in the
centre would have allowed this lamp to be hung from
the ceiling. It rests on a short round foot while the body
is richly decorated with three winged heads.

美少年灯座

青铜
公元 1 世纪
150cm × 60cm × 60cm

Statue of an ephebe lamp holder

Bronze
1st century AD
150cm × 60cm × 60cm

住宅和花园装饰
Domus and Garden Décor

花园是古罗马房屋中最重要的空间之一。古罗马人在花园度过一天的大部分时间。天气好的时候，他们喜欢到户外散步或在树荫下休息、阅读、写诗、讨论哲学或政治。

花园通常是精心打理的，里面有着令人印象深刻的建筑和装饰元素。花园也是自我表现的重要媒介，是展示文化和财富的理想之地。此外，花园还发挥至关重要的实用功能，在拥挤和混乱的城市环境中提供良好的光源和新鲜的空气，而鲜花和芳香植物的气味能掩盖外面传来的持久的、令人不快的气味。

花园的装饰通常受到神话和戏剧的启发，尤其受到酒神游行文化的启发。酒神狄俄尼索斯在古希腊文化中象征着奢华、富裕、原始自然和户外生活的乐趣。

The garden was one of the most important rooms in the Roman home. In the garden the Romans spent a good part of the day. In fine weather they loved to stroll in the open air or relax in the shade of a tree to read, write poetry, discuss philosophy or politics.

Gardens, usually well-kept and laid out with impressive architectural and decorative elements, were also an important means of displaying one's culture and wealth to the world. They also served a critically important practical function, providing, in crowded and chaotic urban settings, a good source of light and fresh air, while the scent of flowers and aromatic plants covered and made any lingering and unpleasant odours from outside more tolerable.

Their decoration was usually inspired by mythical and theatrical themes but especially by the Dionysian world to celebrate Dionysus as the god of Hellenistic *tryphè* (luxury, pageantry), wild nature, and the joy of the outdoors.

诸神使者墨丘利雕像

青铜
公元 1 世纪
17cm × 11cm

这是一尊墨丘利的青铜小雕像。底座为圆柱形。墨丘利神是商人、财富所有者和旅行者的保护神。雕像中的墨丘利呈站姿，左腿弯曲、脸侧向右边。他的胸前披着古罗马式的短斗篷，斗篷在左臂上打成结，并没有盖在身上，身上的其余部位裸露着。墨丘利神头上戴着植物冠，中央有一枚竖直的叶子。他伸出的右手拿着一个装满钱的钱袋，这是收入丰厚的象征；垂下的左手拿着象征自己的墨丘利之杖，上面盘踞着两条蛇。蛇身下方是一双翅膀，从神杖两边伸开。它们是速度的象征——正是速度让墨丘利的旅行更佳便捷。

Figurine of Mercury

Bronze
1st century AD
17cm × 11cm

Bronze figurine of Mercury, placed on a cylindrical base. The god, protector of merchants, earnings and travellers, is represented standing, with his left leg bent, his face turned to the right. He wears a cloak (chlamys) on his chest, then wrapped around his left arm, detached from his body; he is otherwise naked. The god's head is crowned with plant elements, and a central vertical leaf. With his outstretched right hand he shows a bag filled with denarii, a symbol of good earnings. With his lowered left hand he holds the caduceus, his specific symbol, consisting of a staff from which two snakes are coiled. Beneath these are two wings, projecting sideways, a symbol of the speed that facilitates travel.

大力神赫丘利雕像

青铜
公元 1 世纪
5cm×6cm

这是一尊赫丘利的青铜小雕像。赫丘利面朝前方，他的左腿微微弯曲，右手放在侧腰位置，左手持着棍棒的一端，另一端搭在肩膀上。棍棒是赫丘利标志性的武器。赫丘利头上覆盖着涅墨亚狮的狮皮。他在最初成为英雄的时候杀死了这只狮子。雕像中，狮爪还绑在他的脖子前面。

众神之王朱庇特雕像

青铜
公元 1 世纪
18cm×7cm

这是一尊朱庇特的青铜小雕像。底座为圆形凹面，上窄下宽。这座立身像中，众神之王朱庇特左腿微屈。他赤裸身体，一件多褶的长斗篷披在左肩上。朱庇特露出正脸，脸上有络腮胡，卷发很浓密。他下垂的右手握着闪电，左脚边立着一只鹰，这正是他力量的象征。

Figurine of Hercules

Bronze
1st century AD
5cm × 6cm

Bronze figurine depicting Hercules. Hercules' stance is frontal, standing, his left leg slightly bent. His right hand is held at hip level, while his left holds the lower end of the club, his characteristic weapon, resting on his shoulder. The demigod's head is covered by the skin of the Nemean lion, slain at the beginning of his career: the legs of the pride are knotted in front of his neck.

Figurine of Jupiter

Bronze
1st century AD
18cm × 7cm

Bronze figurine of Jupiter placed on a concave circular base tapering at the bottom. The father and lord of all gods is represented standing, with his left leg flexed. The body is nude, a long cloak also rests on the left shoulder and falls from it in wide folds. The face of the god is in perspective, bearded, with a rich, curly hair. In his right hand lowered to his side he holds the thunderbolt, while the eagle, his symbol of power, is placed near his left foot.

守护神拉尔雕像

青铜
公元 1 世纪
19cm × 7cm

拉尔是保护家族成员的神祇，确保着他们的健康和家族的繁荣。拉尔们通常的形象是一只手拿着来通杯，另一只手拿着供奉盘。

Figurine of a Lar

Bronze
1st century AD
19cm × 7cm

The lar was a household deity that protected the members of the family, ensuring their health and prosperity. They are often depicted with the following attributes: a rhyton (drinking vessel) in one hand, and a patera (offering dish) in the other.

守护神拉尔雕像

青铜
公元 1 世纪
27cm × 10cm

这位拉尔神一手拿着来通杯，另一只手拿着供奉盘。他
被描绘成运动中的形象，斗篷在身后飘动。他正迈出一
步，可能是舞蹈中的一步。

Figurine of a Lar

Bronze
1st century AD
27cm × 10cm

This lar deity holds a rhyton (drinking vessel) in one hand
and a patera (offering dish) in the other. He is depicted in
movement, with his cloak flowing behind him, as he takes,
possibly dancing, a step.

有女海妖斯库拉的水盆

斑岩
公元 1 世纪
98cm × 100cm × 92cm

斑岩是一种罕见且坚硬的紫红色岩石，因其独特的颜色而在古典时代受到高度重视。紫色被认为是帝王的颜色，因此斑岩被视为皇家宝石。由于坚硬而难以开采，又需要从原产地埃及运出，斑岩成为象征着等级和权威的奢侈材料。这个水盆应该曾位于精英人士的花园中，上面雕刻的是古代神话中超自然的女海妖斯库拉，其细节体现着做工的精美。

Garden water basin with Scylla

Porphyry
1st century AD
98cm × 100cm × 92cm

Porphyry is a rare and hard, purple-red stone that was highly prized in antiquity for its distinct colour. Purple was considered an imperial colour, and thus porphyry was regarded as a royal stone. The need to transport it from Egypt where it was found, and the difficulty in quarrying it due to its hardness, made it into a luxury material and symbolized rank and authority. This water basin would have been located in a garden of the elite and the beautiful craftsmanship can be seen in the detailing of Scylla, a supernatural female sea monster found in ancient mythology.

有女妖的水盆

大理石
公元 1 世纪
135cm × 108cm

这个大理石水盆由三名鸟身兽爪的女妖托起。水盆中央有另一个从莨苕叶苞里顶出来的叶丛形状的支柱。水盆坐落在高高的三角面大理石底座上，每一侧均为凹面。各面由沟壑状的壁柱线条连接，而凹面则由浅浮雕图案装饰。上层是一圈浮雕饰带，下层则是爱奥尼式树叶形态的饰带。

Labrum with harpies

Marble
1st century AD
135cm×108cm

Marble basin supported by three winged harpies with feral legs. In the centre is a further support in the form of a tuft of leaves springing from an acanthus bud. The basin is placed on a tall support, also made of marble, with a triangular plan and concave sides. The connection between the sides is marked by a kind of fluted pilaster, while the side panels are decorated with low figured reliefs. The upper cornice bears a frieze of astragals, while the lower one bears a frieze of Ionic leaves.

有铁匠图案的浮雕圆盘

大理石
公元 1 世纪
28cm × 3cm

这件大理石圆盘有着双面浮雕装饰，曾悬挂于花园作为装饰之用。
圆盘正面是一名铁匠，他正用一对长钳将一个不明器物放在窑上。
圆盘背面是一名坐着的铁匠，他正在铁砧上锤打一块不明的器物。

Oscillum with blacksmith

Marble
1st century AD
28cm × 3cm

Marble disc with relief decoration on both faces. It was used
suspended as a decorative element in the garden. On face A a
blacksmith is depicted holding an unidentifiable object on the
anvil, held by a pair of long tongs. On face B a blacksmith is
represented seated while hammering an unidentifiable object
on the anvil.

大理石
公元 1 世纪
28cm × 5cm

Oscillum with Medusa head

Marble
1st century AD
28cm × 5cm

有海怪及女子图案的浮雕圆盘

大理石
公元 1 世纪
28cm × 3cm

Oscillum with female figure on marine monster

Marble
1st century AD
28cm × 3cm

115

有少年与海豚的喷泉嘴

大理石
公元 1 世纪
42cm × 36cm × 24cm

Fountain mouth in the shape of a youth with dolphin

Marble
1st century AD
42cm × 36cm × 24cm

宁芙与萨提尔

大理石
公元 1 世纪
122cm × 70cm × 65cm

在这座展现萨提尔和宁芙仙女的大理石雕
像组中，萨提尔坐在一块石头上，用左臂
环抱住宁芙的上身，将她搂到身前，宁芙
的衣衫滑落。尽管这组雕像遭受的风化作
用及其缺失的部分让人难以完整欣赏到人
物的姿势，却并不影响人们感受姿态中欲
说还休的妩媚风情。

Satyr and nymph

Marble
1st century AD
122cm × 70cm × 65cm

Marble statue depicting a satyr and
a nymph. The satyr, seated on a rock,
encircles with his left arm the torso
of the nymph, unclothed, drawing her
towards him. The corrosion and lacunae
from which the group suffers no longer
allow us to fully appreciate the gestures
of the two figures, but do not prevent us
from still grasping the agitated, and at
the same time voluptuous, rhythm of the
representation.

有酒神像的柱子

大理石
公元 1 世纪
64cm × 15cm × 14cm

这类矩形石柱的顶端以头像作为收束。有头像的石柱最早来自古希腊人，他们会设置有赫耳墨斯神头像的柱子，以标记土地的边界和十字路口。在古罗马时代，头像扩展至多样的内容：萨提尔、酒神女信徒、年轻运动员、哲学家和神等，而且也用于家庭装饰。

Herm with Dionysus

Marble
1st century AD
64cm × 15cm × 14cm

Herms are rectangular stone shafts terminating in a head. The origin comes from the Greeks, who would place pillars surmounted by the head of the god Hermes to mark boundaries and crossroads. During Roman times they depicted various subjects; satyrs, maenads, young athletes, philosophers, gods, and would have been used for decorative purposes around the home.

公元 1 世纪

112cm × 20cm × 18cm

Herm with Dionysus

Marble

1st century AD

112cm × 20cm × 18cm

公元 1 世纪

235cm × 27cm × 9cm

Decorative partition

Fresco

1st century AD

235cm × 27cm × 9cm

花园装饰画

壁画
公元 1 世纪
19cm × 36.5cm × 5cm

这件灰泥墙面彩绘装饰画有着黄橙色的背景，
上面绘有鸟类、昆虫和树叶图案。

Garden fresco

Fresco
1st century AD
19cm × 36.5cm × 5cm

A painted wall plaster with birds, insects and leaves on a yellow-orange background.

壁画

花园装饰画

壁画
公元 1 世纪
38.5cm × 42.5cm × 5.5cm

这幅壁画描绘了一只向上看的鸟。画面右侧有四朵带白色花瓣的花。

Garden fresco

Fresco
1st century AD
38.5cm × 42.5cm × 5.5cm

This wall painting depicts a bird looking upwards. To the right of the composition are four flowers with white petals.

风景画

壁画
公元 1 世纪
34cm × 34.5cm × 5.5cm

这是一幅景观壁画，前景中有建筑元素、树木和人物，背景为橙色。

Landscape painting

Fresco
1st century AD
34cm × 34.5cm × 5.5cm

A landscape wall painting with an architectural element, trees and figures in the foreground on an orange background.

风景画

风景画

壁画
公元 1 世纪
50cm × 41cm × 5.5cm

这是一幅景观壁画，前景中有建筑元素、树木和
人物。背景中描绘的山脉使画面显得更为深邃。

Landscape painting

Fresco
1st century AD
50cm × 41cm × 5.5cm

A landscape wall painting with an architectural
element, trees and figures in the foreground. In
the background are mountains, creating a field
of depth.

古代艺术中美的概念
The Concept of Beauty in Ancient Art

在历史的长河中，围绕美的观念，人类发展出了许多概念。在古代美学中就有和谐、对称、韵律、协调等。比起审美，它们更与道德相关。

古希腊人将美的概念与优雅和尺度，尤其是和比例的概念联系在一起。当身体的所有部分达到平衡、对称和和谐时，身体就是美丽的。美是形状的完美比例，也是内在和谐的反映。理想的古希腊男人是英俊而有美德的。裸体是英雄的标志，是身心俱佳的象征。

作为和谐的美表达着一个人的道德层面。一切吸引和引起我们钦佩其辉煌的事物，值得最高的尊重。美也表达着一个人的谦逊和平衡，即睿智。

从这个角度来看，艺术和建筑作品也深受启发，通过各部分清晰和精确的比例追求对称和完美。

Throughout history man has developed many ideas around the idea of beauty: in ancient aesthetics we speak of harmony, symmetry, and eurythmy to which ethical rather than aesthetic virtues are associated.

With the idea of beauty the ancient Greeks associated the concepts of grace, measure and above all proportion: a body is beautiful when there is balance, symmetry and harmony among all its parts. Beauty is the perfect proportion of forms but also a reflection of inner harmony. The ideal Greek man is beautiful and virtuous. The naked body is the distinctive mark of the hero, a symbol of physical and moral excellence.

Beauty expresses the moral dimension of a man: anything that attracts and arouses our admiration for its splendour is also worthy of the highest esteem. Being beautiful also expresses a man's ability to be moderate and balanced, in other words, wise.

With this in mind, artistic and architectural productions were also inspired by the quest for symmetry and perfection achieved through clear and precise proportions of individual parts.

海伦：世间绝色
Helen: the Most Beautiful of Mortal Women

特洛伊国王普里阿摩斯在"白臂海伦"出现时低语道："貌似天仙"（《伊利亚特》，III 158）。海伦是勒达和宙斯的女儿，因为半神的身份而美丽，更被认为是"世间最美丽的女人"。她代表着卓越的理想女性形象。美是一种神赐的礼物，它使人与神相似，但同时，它本身也具有很大的宿命性，可以显露出不幸的底色。

事实上确实如此，海伦的命运就是以帕里斯的评判为标志的。这位年轻的牧羊人在一场女性的比赛中被选为裁判，以决定赫拉、雅典娜和阿佛洛狄忒中谁是最美丽的女神。三位女神争相承诺，将用"礼物"回报帕里斯。牧羊人最终接受了阿佛洛狄忒的礼物，因为阿佛洛狄忒曾答应他会娶到世界上最美丽的女人海伦。而海伦也的确与帕里斯偷情，由此引发了特洛伊战争。

海伦对男人的魅惑力是巨大的。同样令人印象深刻的是，她给这个世界带来无数死亡与毁灭，用自己的魅惑颠倒了众生的命运。正如我们所见，神赐的美丽同时带有积极和消极的意义。

"Wondrously like is she to the immortal goddesses" (Iliad, III 158). Daughter of Leda and Zeus, beautiful by semi-divine nature but also considered "the most beautiful of all women", she embodies the feminine ideal par excellence. Beauty is a gift of divine origin, making men similar to the gods, but at the same time, possessing within itself a good dose of fatality that can prove to bring misfortune.

Indeed, Helen's fate is marked by the events that follow the judgment of Paris, the young shepherd chosen to decide which of Hera, Athena, and Aphrodite is the most beautiful. The three goddesses compete by promising their "gifts" to Paris. He accepts the gift of Aphrodite, who had promised him in marriage the most beautiful woman in the world, Helen, who becomes an adulteress against her will and the trigger for the Trojan War.

The fascination exercised by Helen on men was enormous, as was the mass of deaths and ruins that she brought to the world, upsetting the lives of men and women. The gift of beauty, as we can see, is full of positive and negative meanings at the same time.

有帕里斯、海伦及阿佛洛狄忒的浮雕

大理石
公元 1 世纪
68cm × 68cm × 7cm

这件雕工精细的浮雕作品刻画了帕里斯评判的场景，在古希腊神话中，这正是特洛伊战争的导火索。最英俊的凡间男子帕里斯在不明就里的情况下，被要求把金苹果交给赫拉、雅典娜和阿佛洛狄忒三位女神之中最美的一位。帕里斯选中了阿佛洛狄忒，激怒了另外两位女神，触发了一系列事件，最终导致特洛伊战争爆发。

Relief with Paris, Helen and Aphrodite

Marble
1st century AD
68cm × 68cm × 7cm

This beautifully crafted relief depicts the judgement of Paris, one of the causes of the Trojan War in Greek mythology. Paris, the most handsome among mortals, was unwittingly asked to give a golden apple to the most beautiful of the goddesses Hera, Athena and Aphrodite. Paris chose Aphrodite, incurring the wrath of the other two and provoking the events that led to the Trojan War.

有海伦诞生图案的红绘双柄大口罐

陶

公元前 4 世纪

36cm × 35cm

这是一个典型的钟形罐。罐身黑色背景上装饰有红色和白色人物形象，描绘了海伦诞生的场景。

Red-figured krater with Helen's birth

Pottery

4th century BC

36cm × 35cm

A classic example of a vase with a particular shape called bell krater. Decorated with red-figures and white, the scene depicts the birth of Helen, located in the middle of the composition.

有海伦和墨涅拉俄斯图案的红绘雅典酒罐

陶
公元前 5 世纪
37cm × 37cm

这种黏土容器在古希腊地区自公元前 6 世纪末期开始生产，在伊特鲁里亚地区一直沿用至公元前 4 世纪，罐身呈球形，矮脚短颈、开口宽大，有横向手柄。这件展品上的装饰描绘了海伦和斯巴达国王墨涅拉俄斯的形象。

Red-figured Stamnos with Helen and Menelaus

Pottery
5th century BC
37cm × 37cm

The Stamnos is a clay vessel produced in Greece from the late 6th century BC and in Etruria until the 4th century BC. It has a globular body, low foot and neck with a wide opening and horizontal handles. The decoration in this example depicts Helen and Menelaus king of Sparta.

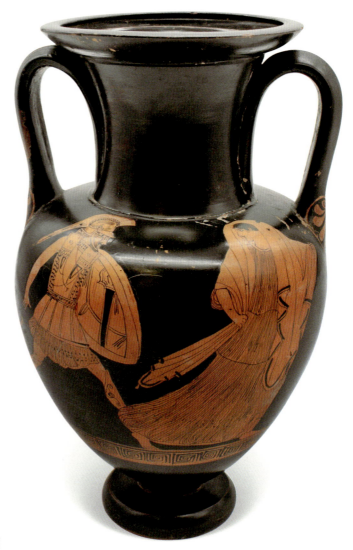

有海伦和墨涅拉俄斯图案的双耳瓶

陶
公元前 5 世纪
34cm × 20cm

这种大双耳瓶用于运输或存放液体。瓶身装饰描绘了海伦和斯巴达国王墨涅拉俄斯的形象。

Amphora with Helen and Menelaus

Pottery
5th century BC
34cm × 20cm

Large vase with two handles used to carry or contain liquids. The decoration depicts Helen and Menelaus, King of Sparta.

古罗马时期的女性形象
The Woman in Roman Times

维苏威火山地区的城市得以将最多的古代壁画装饰留存给今天的人们。这些壁画中有许多女性角色：女神、女英雄、女祭司、仆人和飞翔的形象。有时她们是刻板的人物，而有时她们的形象则带着明确的现实意味以及与日常生活的联系。

像在今天一样，即使在古罗马时期，女性的发型设计方式也千差万别。不可否认，发型能赋予人很大一部分美感。然而，在古罗马文明的最早时期，一直到公元前 1 世纪，男性和女性的发型都非常简单。

从公元前 1 世纪末开始，引领时尚的帝国公主们的发型变得越来越复杂。在朱里亚 – 克劳狄王朝（公元 1 世纪上半叶），十分常见的是宽大的波浪发型；而在弗拉维王朝间（公元 1 世纪末），女性将头发设计成非常复杂的卷发。公元 2 世纪开始，她们则广泛使用假发和发套。

The vesuvian cities have returned the greatest amount of pictorial wall decorations that the ancient world could leave us. Female characters appear in many of them: goddesses, heroines, priestesses, servants and flying figurines. Sometimes they are stereotypical figures, but other times their depiction has a clear realistic intent and a connection to everyday life.

Just like nowadays, the way women's hair was styled in Roman times was extremely varied. The hair is undeniably entrusted with a large part of an individual's beauty; however, in the earliest period of Rome's civilization and up to the first century BC, hairstyles, both male and female, were extremely simple.

From the end of the first century B.C. the hairstyles of imperial princesses, who dictated fashion, would become increasingly complex. In the Julio-Claudian era (first half of the first century AD) wide wavy hairstyles are very common, while in the Flavian era (late first century AD) women had their hair styled in complicated curls, leading up to the adoption of hairpieces and wigs widely in use from the second century AD onward.

有女子妆扮图案的红绘双耳细颈罐

陶
公元前 4 世纪
29cm × 21cm

这种敞口罐用于储存液体，罐体向下扩宽，有两个带状手柄。黑底上的红绘装饰描绘了女子梳妆的场景。

Red-figured Pelike with grooming scene

Pottery
4th century BC
29cm × 21cm

The pelike is a type of vessel with a wide mouth. Used to hold liquids, it has the widest part towards the bottom and two vertical ribbon-like handles. The red figures on a black background here depict a female grooming scene.

有告别逝者（女子梳妆打扮）图案的
双涡形柄大口罐

陶
公元前 4 世纪
62cm×37cm

这种造型独特的大口罐来自意大利南部的阿普
利亚地区，具有扁平的边缘、宽敞的喇叭状瓶
颈以及卵形罐身。两侧粗大的手柄末端各有一
个面具装饰。罐身装饰画呈现了告别逝者的场
景，其中女性人物形象的发型和服饰描绘特别
丰富。

Volute krater with greeting to the deceased

Pottery
4th century BC
62cm × 37cm

This is a particular type of vase from southern
Italy, Apulia. It has a flat rim and a wide
flared neck and an ovoid bod. The wide side
handles end with two decorated masks. The
decoration shows a scene of greeting to the
deceased. The depiction of women's hairstyles
and clothing is particularly detailed.

有赫斯珀里得斯花园的红绘细颈有柄长瓶

陶
公元前 4 世纪
46cm × 28cm

这种瓶子长身细颈，具有单手柄和宽大的喇叭状边缘。其主要用途是储存和倾注香油和香膏，通常为运动员所使用，也常用于葬礼。这件展品有红绘装饰，描绘了赫斯珀里得斯花园。这座花园里有宙斯送给赫拉的礼物——一棵金苹果树。赫拉克勒斯的十二伟业之一，就是到赫斯珀里得斯花园摘取三个金苹果。

Red-figured Lekythos with the Garden of the Hesperides

Pottery
4th century BC
46cm × 28cm

The lekhythos is a long-bodied vase with a narrow neck, a single handle and a wide flared rim. It had the main function of storing and pouring perfumed oils and ointments and was therefore mainly used by athletes and in funeral ceremonies. This specimen contains a red-figure decoration depicting the Garden of the Hesperides. A gift from Zeus to Hera, an apple tree with golden fruit grew in the garden. It was also the scene of one of the labours of Hercules who was ordered to pick three golden apples.

有女子妆扮图案的红绘女性风格提水罐

陶
公元前 4 世纪
47cm×33cm

Red-figured Hydria with grooming scene

Pottery
4th century BC
47cm × 33cm

有女子妆扮图案的红绘提水罐

陶
公元前 4 世纪
43cm × 37cm

这是一种古希腊陶罐，主要用于提水，有时也用作骨灰瓮和投票箱。它的颈部修长，有三个手柄，其中两个安装在罐身最宽敞的位置，第三个安装在瓶颈处，以便于倒水。这种造型源自克里特岛，广泛使用于整个古希腊 - 古罗马地区。这件展品上带有红绘装饰，描绘了女性梳妆的场景。

Red-figured Hydria with grooming scene

Pottery
4th century BC
43cm × 37cm

The hydria is a Greek vessel used mainly for carrying water but also as a cinerary urn and sometimes as a religious votive. It has a pronounced neck and three handles. Two mounted on the widest part of the body, the third on the neck to facilitate the pouring of water. The form, originating from Crete, spread throughout the Greco-Roman world. In this specimen, the red-figure depiction contains scenes related to women's grooming.

有女舞者图案的细颈有柄长瓶

陶
公元前 4 世纪
28cm × 13cm

这种瓶子长身细颈，具有单手柄和宽大的喇叭状边缘。其主要用途是储存和倾注香油和香膏，通常为运动员所使用，也常见于葬礼。这件展品上有红绘装饰，描绘了舞者们的形象。

Lekythos with dancer

Pottery
4th century BC
28cm × 13cm

The lekythos is a long-bodied vase with a narrow neck, a single handle and a wide flared rim. It had the main function of storing and pouring perfumed oils and ointments and was therefore mainly used by athletes and in funerary ceremonies. This specimen contains a red-figure decoration depicting dancers.

披着布衣的女子雕像

大理石
公元 2 世纪
212cm × 80cm × 47cm

这是一尊女性大理石雕像。她身穿一件有皱褶的及足长袍，上面披着一件大斗篷。她的右臂弯曲放在胸前。这是典型的谦逊女性形象塑造手法。

Female draped figure

Marble
2nd century AD
212cm × 80cm × 47cm

Marble statue of a female figure. She wears a pleated robe down to her feet, on which is a large cloak hanging. Her right arm is bent and resting on her chest. The depiction is typical of female figures who were depicted as symbols of modesty.

阿格里皮娜雕像

大理石
公元 1 世纪
38cm × 30cm × 30cm

这尊头像再现了阿格里皮娜皇后的容貌，着重突出了她的发型。阿格里皮娜在罗马帝国第一个王朝——儒略 - 克劳狄王朝中扮演着举足轻重的角色，事实上，她是罗马史上第一位兄长、丈夫和儿子都是王子的女性，这种身份把她带到了政治舞台的中心，让她既享受到大显身手的机会，也承受着巨大的风险，例如面临古罗马针对女性的典型指控——无礼和投毒。

Agrippina portrait

Marble
1st century AD
38cm × 30cm × 30cm

The head reproduces the features of the Empress Agrippina with particular emphasis on the hairstyle of her hair. The figure of Agrippina is central to the history of the first Roman imperial dynasty, the Julio-Claudian; she was in fact the first matron to find herself in the condition of sister, wife and mother of a prince, a condition that brought her to the centre of the political scene, of which she fully experienced both the possibilities and the risks, exemplified in the classic accusations levelled against women in Rome, impudence and vengeance.

朱里亚 - 克劳狄王朝公主雕像

大理石
公元 1 世纪
60cm × 36cm × 26cm

这尊雕像描绘了儒略 - 克劳狄王朝的典型发型。王朝初期简单、朴素而整洁的发型让位于更柔和的造型，减轻了原有的严肃感，在太阳穴末端、耳前位置增添了发卷，有时会让几绺头发披散于颈部。这位女子还在发型上装饰了一串珠链。

Portrait of a Julio-Claudian princess

Marble
1st century AD
60cm × 36cm × 26cm

This statue depicts a hairstyle typical of the Julio-Claudian dynasty. The simple austere and neat hairstyles of the beginning of the dynasty made way to softer forms, lightened of its original severity, with the addition of soft curls at the end of temples, in front of ears and sometimes small locks of hair would be loose on the neck. This woman also decorated her hairstyle with a string of beads.

弗拉维王朝贵妇雕像

大理石
公元 1 世纪
71cm × 37cm × 34cm

这尊贵妇头像的发型十分精致，一头发卷
浓厚紧致。后脑环绕的细密麻花辫成为她
的头饰，而前面蓬松的发卷就像一顶帽子。
她很有可能是一位贵妇，或者是一位富有
的自由民的妻子。

Noblewoman from the Flavian dynasty

Marble
1st century AD
71cm × 37cm × 34cm

Portrait of a noblewoman with an
elaborate hairstyle of tight, thick ringlets.
Behind the nape of her neck she is
encircled by close braids that act as a
headdress, while the backcombed curls in
front almost act as a hat. She is most likely
an aristocrat, unless she is the wife of an
enriched freedman.

维斯塔贞女像

大理石
公元 2 世纪
58cm × 32cm × 25cm

维斯塔贞女是罗马灶神维斯塔的女祭司，她们守护着古罗马广场上的维斯塔圣火，并举行其他仪式。维斯塔贞女可以通过面纱识别，她们的面纱以胸针固定，就像新娘的头纱。

Portrait of a Vestal

Marble
2nd century AD
58cm × 32cm × 25cm

The Vestal Virgins were priestesses of Vesta, the goddess of the hearth, who guarded the Vesta flame in the Roman Forum and carried out ceremonies. The Vestal Virgins can be identified by their veils, often fastened with a brooch, similar to a bride's veil.

古风女子头像

大理石
公元 1 世纪
36cm × 25cm × 23cm

Archaic female head

Marble
1st century AD
36cm × 25cm × 23cm

持卷轴的女子像

壁画
公元 1 世纪
26.5cm × 16cm × 4cm

Female figure with rotulus

Fresco
1st century AD
26.5cm × 16cm × 4cm

裹有布衣的女子像

壁画
公元 1 世纪
45cm×24cm×5cm

Female draped figure

Fresco
1st century AD
45cm × 24cm × 5cm

有女子妆扮图案的银水罐

银

公元 3 世纪

55cm×30cm

银水罐是用于奠酒的器皿，通常呈桶形，并带有环形手柄。本展品中的手柄至今仍然固定在水罐上。罐身上描绘了女性妆扮的场景。

Situla

Silver

3rd century AD

55cm×30cm

Situlae are vessels used for libations and are usually found in the shape of a bucket with a loop handle which can be seen in this example still affixed. The scene is related to women's grooming.

有女子妆扮图案的双耳大饮杯

陶

公元前 4 世纪

19cm×30cm

大饮杯是一种饮酒器皿，形状很适于饮酒者持在手中。这件漂亮的展品绘有红色和白色的人物图案：两位女子站在喷泉旁的花园里，进行着日常的打扮，或是在为一场宴会做准备。

Skyphos with grooming scene

Pottery

4th century BC

19cm × 30cm

A skyphos is a drinking vessel, shaped to easily fit the drinkers hand. This beautiful example contains red and white figures; two women are standing in a garden by the fountain, intent on getting ready for the day or even for a banquet.

有婚礼图案的细颈有柄长瓶

陶

公元前 4 世纪

32cm × 11cm

这件有着窄颈、单柄和宽喇叭口的细长瓶上，使用红绘技法描绘了婚礼场景。

Lekythos with wedding scene

Pottery

4th century BC

32cm × 11cm

This lekythos with its long body, narrow neck, single handle and a wide flared rim depicts a wedding scene made with the red-figure technique.

有对话（化妆用品及首饰）图案的双涡形柄大口罐

陶

公元前 4 世纪

45cm × 34cm

这种大口罐是以其手柄命名的，容器顶部边缘的手柄末端有着涡形装饰。这种罐子通常极为精致，有丰富的装饰。这件展品描绘了带有首饰图案的梳妆及谈话场景。左边的人物可能还拿着一个放油膏的香脂瓶。

Volute krater with grooming and conversation scene with jewellery

Pottery

4th century BC

45cm×34cm

The volute krater gives its name to the handles, which end in volutes at the top of the rim of the vessel. They are often particularly elaborated and richly decorated. This example depicts a grooming and conversation scene with jewellery; the figure on the left is may also be holding an unguentarium for ointments.

有对话（化妆用品及首饰）图案的双耳细颈罐

陶
公元前 4 世纪
48cm × 32cm

双耳细颈罐是一种带有宽口的容器，用来盛装液体。这件展品有下垂的罐肚，两侧各有一个垂直的带状手柄。黑色背景上，用红色绘成的人物正在交谈，右边的人物则将一面镜子举在脸前。

Red-figure pelike with grooming and conversation scene with jewellery

Pottery
4th century BC
48cm × 32cm

The pelike is type of vessel with a wide mouth. Used to hold liquids, it has a sagging belly and a vertical ribbon-like handles on either side. The red-figures on a black background here are in conversation; the figure on the right is holding a mirror to her face.

有婚礼（化妆用品及首饰）图案的婚庆罐

陶
公元前 4 世纪
37cm×20cm

婚庆罐是一种用于结婚仪式的古老容器，因此经常绘有婚礼场景，并且带有大的碗状罐体和两个从边缘顶部突出的弯曲手柄。这件展品上有红色的人物形象以及白色绘就的细节。

Lebes gamikos with wedding scene

Pottery
4th century BC
37cm × 20cm

Lebes gamikos is an ancient vessel used in marriage ceremonies and thus often depicts nuptial scenes. It has a large bowl-like body and two curved handles protruding from the top of the rim. This example has red-figures with white detailing.

有告别逝者图案的提水罐

陶
公元前 4 世纪
45cm × 35cm

提水罐是一种主要用于运水的容器，但也用作骨灰瓮，有时还用作投票箱。它有着明显的颈部和三个手柄。其中两个手柄安装在罐身最宽的部位，第三个安装在罐颈上，以便倒水。在本件展品中，中心人物坐在一个精心装饰的爱奥尼亚柱式神庙中，这是一座呈神殿入口形的墓碑。两位女子分立两侧。场景中还描绘着珠宝盒和项链等日常生活用品。人物以红色绘就，墓碑则为白色，以此彰显中央的重要人物，同时起到装饰性的对比效果。

Hydria with greeting to the deceased

Pottery
4th century BC
45cm × 35cm

The hydria is a vessel used mainly for carrying water but also as a cinerary urn and sometimes as a political ballot box. It has a pronounced neck and three handles. Two mounted on the widest part of the body, the third on the neck to facilitate the pouring of water. On this example the central figure sits in an elaborately adorned ionic naiskos, a tombstone in the shape of an entrance to a shrine. Two women flank her on either side. Objects of everyday life are also included in the scene such a jewellery box and a necklace. The figures are red while the tombstone is white, emphasizing the important figure within it and providing a decorative contrast.

女性美容工具
The Tools of Beauty

书面和考古资料向我们提供了有关个人护理和女性美容的丰富信息。古代的作家根据优劣将当时的化妆品进行区分。优质化妆品的药性保持身体的自然；劣质化妆品则提供人造的美感。

古罗马人通过面膜和香膏等化妆品来护理皮肤。也有化妆品以罐装粉末的形式销售，供人们取所需数量调和使用。扇贝的壳也可以成为一种特殊的化妆品容器，粉末状物质或软膏被放置在一侧的贝壳中，另一侧的贝壳则像盖子一样起到封闭作用。

古罗马人不使用玻璃镜子，而是使用或圆或方的、配有手柄的金属（青铜或银质）镜子。在头发护理和造型方面，他们使用骨质或象牙的梳子和发簪。固定更复杂的发型时普遍会用到发簪，发簪末端通常有立体的装饰。

Written and archaeological sources inform us abundantly about uses related to personal care and female grooming. Ancient authors distinguished between good cosmetics, that is, the part of medicine aimed at preserving the body its naturalness, from bad cosmetics, which procures an artificial beauty.

Cosmetics dealt with skin care through masks and ointments. There were also makeup products, usually marketed in the form of powders contained in jars, to be taken in the desired amount and mixed. A special type of cosmetic vessel consisted of shells of the genus *pecten*, where the powdered substance or ointment was placed in one valve and covered with the other.

The Romans did not use glass mirrors, but rather metal mirrors made of bronze or silver of round or square shape, equipped with a handle, while combs and pins made of bone or ivory were used for hair care and styling. To secure more complex hairstyles, the use of pins, the ends of which were often decorated, was quite common.

有植物元素的镜子

银
公元 1 世纪
21cm × 12cm

Mirror with nature motifs

Silver
1st century AD
21cm × 12cm

镜子

银
公元 1 世纪
20cm

镜面微微凸起，应该是经过高度打磨，以提供良好的反射效果。镜子的手柄已丢失，它本应安装在黑色标记所示的地方。镜子背面有三个同心圆环，边缘则装饰着心型螺旋和圆点图案。

Mirror

Silver
1st century AD
20cm

The front of the mirror is slightly convex and would have been highly polished in order to provide a good reflection. A handle is missing, it would have been attached where now the black mark remains. The disc contains three concentric rings, while the rim is decorated with a pattern of heart shaped volutes and dots.

梳子

骨
公元 1 世纪
4cm × 8cm

Comb

Bone
1st century AD
4cm × 8cm

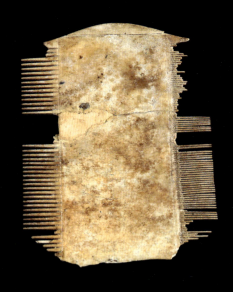

发簪（一套五支）

骨
公元 1 世纪
最长 17cm

Hair pin (set of 5)

Bone
1st century AD
Max length 17cm

化妆品杯

玻璃

公元 1 世纪

4cm × 7cm

这是一个小型的杯状玻璃容器，用于盛放
化妆品。

Cosmetics cup

Glass

1st century AD

4cm × 7cm

Small glass container made in the shape
of a cup to hold cosmetics.

化妆品杯

玻璃

公元 1 世纪

4cm × 7cm

这是一个小型的杯状化妆品容器，具有平
坦的底座和弧形的杯身。

Cosmetics cup

Glass

1st century AD

4cm × 7cm

A small container for cosmetics shaped
like a cup, with a flat base and curved
body.

化妆品盒

玻璃
公元 1 世纪
4cm×9cm

这件展品为圆柱状玻璃容器，很可能用于盛放化妆品或珠宝首饰。其边缘略微突出，底座平坦，便于抓取和放置在物体表面。

Pyxis for cosmetics

Glass
1st century AD
4cm × 9cm

A cylindrical container made of glass, most likely used to hold cosmetics or even trinkets and jewellery. The rim is slightly protruding, and the base is flat, making it easy to grab and put down on surfaces.

镊子

青铜
公元 1 世纪
8cm

这是一把青铜镊子，以一块金属在中点处折叠而成。古代镊子的功能与形状与现代镊子大同小异。

Tweezers

Bronze
1st century AD
8cm

A pair of bronze tweezers made from one piece of metal curved at the mid-point. The function and shape of ancient tweezers are much the same as that of contemporary times.

贝壳盏

银

公元 1 世纪

8cm × 25cm

这个银质小杯盏是一款特别的化妆品容器，状如扇贝。其中一扇贝壳用于盛放脂粉，另一扇贝壳则为盖子。

Cup in the shape of a shell

Silver

1st century AD

8cm × 25cm

This silver cup is a special cosmetics container shaped like a shell of the genus *pecten*. One valve of the shell would have contained the powdered substance or ointment, which was then covered with the other valve.

擦洗皮肤用具（一对）

银
公元 1 世纪
25cm × 15cm

这是一对挂在圆环上的擦洗皮肤用具，具有此种器具典型的钩爪造型。古罗马时代的洗浴程序和个人卫生习惯包括用油清洁身体。在抹油之后，人们会用这种刮刀将多余的油连同死皮和污垢一起刮走。运动员也会在运动之后用它清除身上的污垢、灰尘和油脂。在古希腊时代，这种用具通常只有运动员使用。而到了古罗马时代，洗浴文化是如此流行，它已成为普罗大众的日常用品。

Strigil (a pair)

Silver
1st century AD
25cm × 15cm

A set of two silver strigils on a ring. They are made in the classic claw-like shape typical of these utensils. Part of the bathing and personal hygiene routine in ancient Roman times involved cleaning the body with oil. Having rubbed the oil in, a strigil was used to scrape away any excess as well as any dead skin and dirt. Athletes also used strigils to remove dirt, dust and oil from their bodies after exercise. In the Greek world, the strigil is most often associated with athletes, but for the Romans, the culture of bathing was so popular that the implement became part of the everyday equipment of ordinary people.

香水
The Perfume

香水有着古老的历史，最初来源于沐浴后使用的精油。它是精英阶层财富的体现，具有异常强大的诱惑力。古时的香水，是从花朵的花瓣或根、地中海灌木丛中的典型植物、香料或水果中提取出来的。

古埃及人是香水的大生产商和出口商。在古罗马时期，坎帕尼亚（意大利半岛南部）也兴起了很多香水生产中心。香水被保存在埃及产的一整块雪花石膏制成的典型细长罐中，以防止香精变质。但雪花石膏价格十分昂贵，因此香水也被保存在各种形状、大小和颜色的陶土容器和吹制玻璃容器中。

香水在使用时可以直接用手指蘸取或适量倒出，一点也不浪费。个人护理还包括身体卫生，古罗马人通常使用公共浴场每天清洗身体。为了使皮肤恢复柔软，必须涂抹香水和香油。

Originating as an addition to oils used after bathing, perfume has ancient origins. An expression of the wealth of elites and a very powerful tool of seduction, perfumes in the ancient world were made from flowers, typical Mediterranean plants, spices or fruits.

Great producers and exporters were the Egyptians although, in Roman times, production centres sprang up in the region of Campania. Perfumes were stored in alabastra, typical elongated jars made in Egypt from a block of alabaster. They prevented the perfumed essence from deteriorating but were very expensive, therefore, they were also produced in terracotta and blown glass of various shapes, sizes and colours.

Perfumed substances were drawn directly with the fingers or poured in modest amounts, without wasting a single drop. Personal care began with body hygiene: the rule was to wash every day, commonly using public baths. To restore softness to the skin, it was essential to apply ointments and scented oil.

香膏罐

青铜

公元 1 世纪

11cm × 8cm

这是一个球形青铜香膏罐、罐底向外张开。罐颈呈凹面、双层罐口。圆形耳柄位于罐肩和罐口之间、造型弧度非常优雅。香膏罐用于盛放清洁身体的香膏，涂抹香膏后用擦洗器具刮去。

Ointment container

Bronze

1ˢᵗ century AD

11cm × 8cm

Bronze container with spherical body on flared foot. Neck with concave profile and double shaped rim. From the shoulder to the rim extend the two handles with a circular section, elegantly curved. It contained balsamic oils, used in body hygiene, which were scraped off by the use of the strigil.

香脂瓶

玻璃
公元 1 世纪
9cm×3cm

这是一个浅蓝色的圆柱形玻璃瓶。瓶身由上而
下变粗、底部为圆形。瓶颈很高、为圆柱形。
瓶口较薄、为向外张开的圆柱形。瓶子的作用
是贮存香脂。

Unguentarium

Glass
1st century AD
9cm × 3cm

Cylindrical ointment container in light blue
glass. The lower part is enlarged and rounded
at the bottom. The neck is tall and cylindrical,
ending in a thin rim flared outwards. Used to
contain balsamic oils.

香脂瓶

玻璃
公元 1 世纪
9cm×2cm

Unguentarium

Glass
1st century AD
9cm × 2cm

香脂瓶

玻璃
公元 1 世纪
9cm × 5cm

这是一个浅蓝色的圆柱形玻璃香脂瓶。瓶身由
上而下变粗，下部为圆形。瓶颈为圆柱形。瓶
子的作用是贮存香脂。

Unguentarium

Glass
1st century AD
9cm × 5cm

Cylindrical ointment jar in light blue glass.
The lower part is enlarged and rounded at the
bottom; the neck is long and cylindrical. Used
to contain balsamic oils.

香脂瓶

银
公元 1 世纪
15cm × 12cm

Unguentarium

Silver
1st century AD
15cm × 12cm

香脂瓶

玻璃
公元 1 世纪

庞贝古城的再现
Pompeii Revisited

维苏威火山是庞贝古城和赫库兰尼姆古城周围最主要的景观。火山曾在公元 79 年爆发。火山喷发伴随着强烈的震动，随后，一团火山蒸汽云直冲云霄，接着，沸腾的岩浆纷纷从天上洒落。

直到不久前，人们还普遍认为维苏威火山喷发于公元 79 年 8 月 24 日。这个日期是在古罗马作家小普林尼（Pliny the Younger）的信件中发现的，他是火山喷发的目击者，并设法从这场灾难中逃脱了出来。只是，这些信件的原件没有被保存下来，幸存下来的只有中世纪时期的副本，其中最早的日期是 9 世纪时记录的 8 月 24 日。然而，各种考古证据表明，维苏威火山是在秋季爆发的，因为被发现的受害者们穿着厚重的衣服，而且遗址中出土了很多（秋天收获的）石榴和核桃，还发现了 10 月 17 日的木炭涂鸦。如今普遍的说法是，维苏威火山爆发于公元 79 年的秋天——也许正是在 10 月 24 日，而"8 月 24 日"的说法可能是中世纪译本中出现的错误。

维苏威火山喷发之时，火山旁的这两座城市的命运并不相同。赫库兰尼姆被炽热的泥浆覆盖，而庞贝则被火山喷出的硫磺烟雾覆盖。猛烈迅速的冲击造成的破坏杀死了仍然留在城市中的庞贝人。火山灰和火山岩屑后来形成了一个约 5 米高的覆盖层，掩埋了整个城市和所有的居民。

随着时间的推移，居民们的尸体腐烂分解，在地上留下空洞。考古发掘过程中，人们将石膏倒入这些空腔，重现了窒息而亡的可怜市民的生前形态。庞贝的生命戛然而止，却为后世留下了一项非凡的考古发现，也将一场繁华盛世，凝结成了一个永恒的梦。

The landscape around Pompeii and Herculaneum is dominated by the volcano Vesuvius, which erupted in 79 AD. The eruption was manifested by strong tremors that were followed by the appearance of a very high cloud of volcanic vapour, which was then followed by scalding rain.

Up until not long ago it was generally understood that Vesuvius erupted on August 24, 79 AD. This date was found in Pliny the Younger's letters who was an eyewitness to the eruption and managed to escape the event. However, no original copies of these letters are preserved, and only survive through copies made in the Middle Ages, of which the earliest from the ninth century states August 24. Various archaeological evidences however point to an autumn eruption: the victims have been found to be wearing heavy clothes, pomegranates and walnuts were prevalent (they are harvested in the autumn) and a charcoal graffito dated October 17 was found. It is now generally understood that Vesuvius erupted in the autumn, perhaps October 24, of the year 79 AD and that August 24 may have been an error in medieval translations.

The fate of the two cities, however, was different: Herculaneum was coated in hot mud, while Pompeii was hit by scorching clouds, which caused damage due to the violence and speed of the impact, killing the Pompeians still remaining in the city. The ash and pumice rain formed a cover about 5 meters high, burying the entire city and its inhabitants.

Over time, the bodies decomposed, thus leaving cavities in the ground. During archaeological excavations plaster was poured into these cavities, restoring the form of the poor inhabitants who had been suffocated in the city. Life ended abruptly, but the event left behind a remarkable archaeological discovery and a prosperous life condensed into an eternal dream.

哪里有什么永恒：

骄阳闪耀过，会沉入大海；

皓月圆满过，亦渐渐消损；

狂风怒吼过，终幻作微息。

NIHIL DVRARE POTEST TEMPORE PERPETVO

CVM BENE SOL NITVIT REDDITVR OCEANO

DECRESCIT PHOEBE QVAE MODO PLENA FVIT

VENERVM FERITAS SAEPE FIT AVRA L[E]VIS

Nothing can endure forever
The sun, after shining brightly, casts itself into the ocean
The moon, which was full just now, decreases
The violence of the winds often becomes a light breeze

年轻女子遗体石膏铸像

石膏
20 世纪初
28cm × 161cm × 62cm

这是一尊现代浇铸的石膏模型，是从火山喷发掩埋的一具女性尸体残腔中取得的。庞贝人因火山喷发散发出的有毒气体而死。喷发时堆积在尸体上的火山灰沉积下来，形成了尸体的外壳。随着时间的推移，尸体已经分解，火山灰固化则使得外壳轮廓得以保存。专家们将石膏注入空腔里，从而还原了那些已然消逝的庞贝居民的形态。

Cast of a young woman

Plaster
Early 20th century
28cm × 161cm × 62cm

Modern plaster cast made from the residual cavity in the volcanic ash cover from the decomposition of a woman's body. The volcanic ash, deposited during the eruption on the bodies of Pompeiians killed by poisonous exhalation, preserved their external forms; over time the body dissolved, so that the ash, consolidated, preserved the silhouettes. Plaster, poured into the cavities, restores the now lost forms of the ancient inhabitants of the city.

年轻女子遗体石膏铸像

Cast of a young woman

庞贝古城的发掘
Pompeii Discovered

中世纪和现代初期，人们对庞贝古城的记忆逐渐消失。1748 年，一位农民因为犁陷入地下而发现了一些古罗马文物。由此，人们开始对该地区进行发掘和研究。发掘工作渐渐推进，于 1763 年发现了包含庞贝城名称的铭文。

赫库兰尼姆古城和庞贝古城是最早被完整挖掘和研究的古城，并且是古希腊罗马时期仅有的、被居民匆忙遗弃而无人返回的古城。此外，它们也是仅有的被掩埋在数米深地下的古城，这使得古城的少数幸存者无法或很难取回有用的物品。而且，庞贝并没有像罗马等其他城市那样得到现代化的发展。在庞贝，时间是凝固的，保留着两千年前这座城市的一切——从建筑结构到众多壁画，从日常使用的珠宝到新鲜出炉的面包。因而，与许多其他古代遗址相比，这座城市是独一无二的。虽然距今非常遥远，但人们仍然能从遗留下的这一切当中，鲜明地感知到古代庞贝居民的日常生活。

发掘出的庞贝古城的广度之大、出土文物的数量之多，使其声名远播整个欧洲，并在此后掀起新古典主义等艺术流派的新风潮。18 世纪的发掘使庞贝重返人间，展现着古罗马人特有的爱与美以及生命力。

Of the ancient city of Pompeii, during the Middle Ages and early modern age, memory was lost until 1748 when a farmer, following the sinking of his plough, found some Roman objects. So began research in the area, slowly arriving in 1763 to the discovery of an epigraph containing the name of the city Pompeii.

Herculaneum and Pompeii were the first ancient cities to be excavated in order to discover them in their entirety and were the only ones from the classical era that were hastily abandoned by their inhabitants who never returned to occupy them. Moreover, they are the only ones to have been buried under meters of cover that prevented, or severely limited, the recovery of useful elements to the survivors. While other cities such as Rome have developed in modern times, Pompeii has not, frozen in time and preserving everything in the city as it was 2,000 years ago, from the architectural structures to the many wall frescoes and everyday jewellery to the shapes of freshly baked bread. It makes this city unique in comparison to many other ancient sites. The perception of an everyday life, distant in time but still apparently perceptible, is heightened by all that was left behind.

The fame of the discoveries made, regarding both the size of the ancient city and the large number of artefacts, spread throughout Europe, later sparking new fashions in art such as Neoclassicism. The eighteenth century excavations once again brought Pompeii back to the world, showing the vitality, love, and beauty that characterized the Roman people.

请笃信：痛终有时，爱必将至。

SI DOLOR AFVERIT CREDE REDIBIT AMOR

As soon as the pain subsides, believe me, love comes back.